HOW
TO CREATE
A SUCCESSFUL SKI LESSON FOR
SENIOR CITIZENS

Herbert K. Naito

508 West 26th Street KEARNEY, NE 68848
402-819-3224
info@medialiteraryexcellence.com

Table of Contents

Something About the Author

He spent 40 years in the medical profession. For fun, he coached skiing for over 20 years. He is a member of the Professional Ski Instructors of America, and is certified in PSIA Alpine Skiing, Level 2; PSIA Adaptive Specialist, Level 1; PSIA Children's Specialist, Level 2; PSIA Children's Trainer, and Senior Specialist, Level 1. Currently he is employed by the Vail Resorts and is presently on the Vail Educational Staff. He was the former Director of the Children's Advanced Training Specialist, and the Express Pre-School Ski School Programs. In addition to this, he has published seven ski books and three books on race, racism and discrimination.

1. *"A Comprehensive Guide for Coaching Children How to Ski"*
2. *"How to Prepare Your Child for Their First Ski Lesson"*
3. *"The Funky Donkey Tells His Story About His First Ski Lesson"*
4. *"Coaching Wacky Raccoon, Children, and Adults About the Fundamentals of Good Sportsmanship"*
5. *"The Hidden Secrets and Treasures of Having Fun at and Around the Ski Slopes and Resorts"*
6. *"How to Create Fun for the Disabled Children on the Ski Slopes"*
7. *"How to Create a Successful Ski Lesson for Senior Citizens"*
8. *"How God Prepared and Inspired me to be a Writer and an Author"* 9. *"Why Racism Still Exists in America with Asian Americans"* 10. *"Princess Liliokalani Doesn't Believe in Racism and Hate Crimes Because She is Colorblind"*

Acknowledgements

I want to graciously thank Carlton Guc for the scrutinizing review of this book, Jennifer Barnwell for her gifted talents with her camera, and Jon Stepelton for his graphic artistry.

VAIL Resorts Staff:

Carlton Guc PSIA Alpine Specialist, Level 3; PSIA Children's Specialist, Level 1; PSIA Senior Specialist, Level 2; Vail Resorts Ed Staff

Local Ski School Photographer:

Jennifer Barnwell   PSIA Alpine, Level I; PSIA Children's Specialist, Level 1

Graphic Artist:

Jon Stepelton   PSIA Alpine, Level 3; PSIA Children's Specialist, Level 2; PSIA; Telemark, Level 3; Alpine, Level 3 Trainer; Vail Resorts Ed Staff This book was supported by a grant from the Dr. and Mrs. Herbert K. Naito Charitable Foundation.

Chapter 1

Introduction

Many sports are lifelong experiences—like alpine skiing. There are many scenarios that may account for this. Continuous participation in alpine skiing past retirement age is a common one. Another, is rejoining the family when the children come of age or because they whole family can now afford the sport. Many times, the families are so busy that they put many sports and hobbies aside on the back burner and try to fulfill those dreams after retirement. There are also situations when the family have accumulated great family friends over the years, and they want to have fun skiing with them.

As one ages, the mind and body begin to falter. Learning the profile of a senior citizen is critical to have a successful lesson. There are many things that we teach children that apply to the senior citizen's lessons, but there are other topics that do not apply (i.e., How strenuous the lessons are, catering to their ailments as a high priority, prioritizing to the many side effects of their medications, and many more issues that are unique to seniors. There are so few books that cater to the needs of the older folks when it comes to training ski coaches how to successfully develop lesson plans that will meet with 100 percent needs of the older students and exceed customer satisfaction. I can name a few outstanding citizens that deserves our special attention and handling. For starters, how about our heroic war veterans? Both men and women have earned the hearts of America with their scars and broken bodies and minds. About 12.9 percent of the veterans have posttraumatic syndrome disorder (PTSD) and it is on a significant rise; it is claimed that 60 percent are under-diagnosed. Likewise, firemen/women and policemen/women have been victims of significant traumas that led to similar clinical conditions and events. These kinds of Seniors certainly deserve better help, treatment, and services. When you receive one of these individuals, be sure to put your best ski coaching skills on the line.

Chapter 2

<u>Definition of Senior Citizen</u>

There is no standard definition of what connotates a senior. You ask a dozen individuals; you will probably get a dozen different answers. You may get a response, "I'm only 45-year-old, but I feel like 85-years-old or I'm 90years-old, but I feel like 35-years old." Age is just a number. According to the Webster's Dictionary, "It's an older person, especially if they are retired." For the purposes of consistency and clarity, let us define senior citizens as any individual that is over 50-years-old in this book.

Photo 1. This is an 80-year-old woman who still loves the sport of skiing and spends once a week participating for exercise.

Photo 2. This is a young couple, 50-years of age, that skis and do a lot of walking in the woods after doing an hour of alpine skiing.

Chapter 3

<u>Common Aliments that Affect Senior Citizens</u>

About 80 percent of seniors have at least one chronic health conditions and 68 percent have two or more. Despite these statistics, older adults can maximize health and quality of life by managing symptoms from existing health actions and reducing the risk of developing other conditions. Fifteen of the most common chronic conditions will be listed along with recognizable symptoms and how it may affect their performance with the sport.

Hypertension[23]

High blood pressure is very common affecting 58% if the seniors. It is defined as a resting blood pressure exceeding 140/90 mmHg (Systolic/diastolic pressure).

Hypertension go hand-in-hand with diabetes and it continues to be a common aliment in seniors all over the world. The reason why they go hand-in hand is because the high sugar in the blood causes the blood vessels to calcify causing the formation of plaques known as atherosclerosis which is known as hardening of the arteries that lead to hypertension.

High blood pressure is a risk factor for heart disease and strokes. Whenever you have a senior with diabetes you not only have to be concerned with his/her diabetes and blood sugar, but also, blood pressure and strokes. The symptoms of hypertension are:

• Mild hypertension: non-symptomatic
• Severe hypertension: severe headaches, nosebleed, fatigue, confusion, vision problems, difficulty breathing. What are the causes of hypertension?
• Obesity
• Alcohol consumption
• Diabetes
• Renal disease

• Sleep apnea
• Diet, if one is salt-sensitive, salt intake will cause hypertension.

There are multitude of pills that will control high-blood pressure. The issue is to be sure to take them daily when there are cognitive impairments.

Obesity[21,23]

The prevalence of obesity in older people has dramatically increased in recent years. In America, more than 30 percent of men and women aged 60 years and over are obese. Many have called this disorder an epidemic condition in the elderly. Seniors no longer have confidence in their physical ability. The seniors have increasing fears of injuring themselves. Healthcare cost of people 65 and older cost Medicare spending 25 percent for five percent of the seniors. In healthy young individuals, 30 percent of the body weight is muscle, 20 percent is adipose tissue, and 10 is bone. By age 75, about 15 percent is muscle, 40 percent is adipose tissue, and 8 percent is bone and bone density progressively declines in the aging person. This loss of bone results in more frequent bone fractures[21].

Connective tissue in ligaments and tendons loses tensile strength, elasticity, and regenerative capacity with aging. These changes may at least partially explain why, with aging, tensile strength, elasticity, and regenerative capacity of ligaments and tendons decrease. Another reason is the decline endocrine system, especially testosterone and thyroxine levels.

The elderly begins to lose interest in physical activity especially with a lost of their companion and friends. Their priority of socializing with their friends with high calorie foods and booze does not help with the cause of gaining weight.

As their senior specialist coach, encourage your guest to indulge in some exercise to build good fitness to help prevent injuries and help reduce the recovery time from injuries. The senior specialist coach can begin by doing *stretching* exercises before the lesson to help reduce the risk of an accident. A strong core, flexibility, and balance training all play a role in injury prevention. The National Institutes of Health recommends four-types of exercises[21] to be built into weekly routines:

• Strength
• Balance
• Stretching
• Endurance

Heart Disease[23]

Cardiac disease is especially common in males with a incident of 47 percent, while females have an incident of slightly less; but now the statistics are beginning to reverse the trend, and women are exceeding men. Coronary heart disease (CHD) risk factors include hypertension, high blood cholesterol and sugar, family history, aging, stress, and lack of exercise, stress. CHD is caused by narrowing of the coronary blood vessels (Atherosclerosis) causing insufficient oxygen to the heart muscle (Myocardium). Heart failure symptoms include:

• Shortness of breath
• Have swollen feet, legs, ankles
• Nagging cough, followed by white or pink mucus, when fluid backs up into the lung
• Confusion or memory loss
• Rapid weight gain
• Feeling tired, fatigued
• Feeling compression of the chest

Arthritis[23]

About 31 percent of the seniors have this bone-joint disease. There are two common types of arthritis: osteoarthritis and rheumatoid arthritis. Among older folks, osteoarthritis is more common, which is caused by wear and tear of the joints. In contrast, rheumatoid arthritis is an autoimmune disease, where the overactive immune system attacks the lining of the bone joints.

Arthritis symptoms include:

• Joint pain, tenderness, and/or stiffness
• Limited range of motion

• Inflammation in and around the joints

Unfortunately, there is currently no cure for arthritis. There are effective painkillers such as corticosteroids and other newly formed arthritis medications yet to be proven to be effective.

Diabetes

About 27 percent of the geriatric population are afflicted by diabetes. There are three types of diabetes:

1. Type 1 Diabetes[29]

The disease starts very early in childhood. The pancreatic cells have been destroyed by the immune system; thus-- it cannot produce enough insulin, which is needed to carry the sugar into the cells for energy. These individuals require exogenous insulin to maintain their carbohydrate metabolism. Too much exogenous insulin results in the blood sugar to rapidly drop, i.e., usually within a few seconds to a few minutes. This *hypoglycemic* condition can result in the following *symptoms*:

• Loss of cognitive function and the person may go into comma or even death if the sugar level in the blood is in the *critical zone* (40-60 mg/dL). If the sugar is between 61-89 mg/dL, just monitor. Ideally, it should be between 90-110 mg/dL. Lesser symptoms include fatigue, irritability, loss of attention, being jittery, sweaty, thirsty.

What can you do?
• Recognize the hypoglycemic symptoms
• Stop what you are doing and immediately take the elderly to the family or the Ski Patrol hut.
• Ask the friend that came with him/her if there are anything special that you should know about grandpa. If he is a diabetic, ask if he had a good meal before of the lesson, if he took his diabetic medications, and did he recently test his blood sugar?
• Do *not* provide sugar if you think that it is a hypoglycemic reaction because your client should be tested for blood sugar level to also rule out a hyperglycemic reaction, which has similar symptoms as hypoglycemia.

2. Type 2 Diabetes[29]

While this form of diabetes can occur in early childhood, it is more common later in childhood, such as during the teen years, and in early adulthood, when overweight and obesity become more rampant. The pancreas still produces the normal amount of insulin, but the body is resistant to it and the insulin cannot attach to the receptor sites on the cell. This inhibits the insulin-carrying sugar from getting into the cell. The pancreas tries to produce more insulin (Over production) in an attempt to correct the situation. Hyperinsulinemia results, with cause many other metabolic problems. The common symptoms include being thirsty, hungry, tired, blurred vision, sweating, irritability, cognitive impairment and frequent urination[29]. As a senior specialist coach, you should plan on making frequent five-minute breaks so the elders can go to the bathroom. The symptoms of high blood sugar (Hyperglycemia) are very similar to hypoglycemia.

While both conditions are important to recognize, hypoglycemia is the more important one to focus on the hill. You can ask the older adult:

• When did you last eat?
• What did you eat?
• Did you take your medication?
• Are you carrying a glucometer?

The blood sugar status of the person is dependent on (1) Insulin, (2) the amount, the kind, and timing of the food intake, and (3) the duration, intensity, and frequency of the physical activity (See figure 1) and the amount of insulin or other glucose-lowering medication taken. Any time the child shifts one of the components in the triangle, i.e., increasing the amount of physical activity (like skiing) or not eating the usual diet, the sugar metabolism will be out of control, resulting in the symptoms described above.

Figure 1. Diabetes Triad[29]

What can you, as a coach do to assist in a hypoglycemic crisis, which is similar to what is listed above under Type 1 or Type 2 diabetes? I focus on the Type 2 diabetes because it is more common, especially in the elderly. You can have a condition called "brittle diabetes" whereby extreme hyperglycemia (In excess of 600 mg/dL) is relative common.

The main thing to acknowledge about diabetes is when the elderly's blood sugar is out of control, especially during hypoglycemia, you must work quickly because the level of cognitive confusion occurs within a few seconds to a couple minutes. Unconsciousness and even death may occur. Since the symptoms of hypoglycemia and hyperglycemia are similar, it is best that the senior citizen visit the ski patrol and get his/her blood tested with a glucometer before being treated.

3. Gestational Diabetes[29]

This form occurs in pregnancy. Since this type does not generally apply to this age group, I will not expand this discussion.

Renal Diseases[23]

About 40 percent of persons 60 years and older have Chronic Kidney Disease (CKD). So, this is a very common ailment, especially if untreated or poorly treated. Many people don't realize that, as we age, we lose kidney function. The National Kidney Foundation urges everyone over the age of 60 years to be screened for kidney disease. Kidney disease often develops slowly with few outward symptoms:

- Nausea
- Vomiting
- Loss of appetite
- Fatigue and weakness
- Sleep problems
- Urinating more
- Decreased mental sharpness
- Muscle cramping
- Swelling of the feet and ankles
- Dry, itchy skin
- Hypertension that's difficult to control
- Shortness of breath, if fluid builds up in the lungs
- Chest pain, if fluid builds up around the lining of the heart

Hypertension[23]

The prevalence of hypertension is high if 74.5 percent among those aged 60 years and older. Poor diet (e.g.,High-salt intake), obesity, lack of exercise and Stress, being a diabetic are common causes that lead to high-blood pressure. There are a multitude of medications to control hypertension. First-line medications are diuretics, which control the plasma volume in the blood. I mention this because like caffeine, they cause frequent urination. So, be mindful to make frequent "pit stops" for your guests who are on diuretics and had one-too many cups of coffee.

Cancer[23]

Did you know that 50 percent of the adults between ages 65-74 years can develop a form of cancer some point in their lives? There are over 200 types of cancers such as lung, prostate, skin, and breast carcinomas. Currently, cancer ranks third in the elderly for deaths from diseases. Here are some common symptoms:
- Unexpected lump
- Unexplained weight loss
- Unexplained blood in the stool, urine, sputum, or vomit

Today, there are multitude of effective treatment modalities. What will be most concerning will be the side effects of the more toxic approaches such as chemotherapy, radiation therapy, and other aggressive approaches of curing cancer. Some of the common presentations that the cancer patients will experience during aggressive cancer therapy:

• Fatigue and tiredness
• Mouth, Gum and throat sores
• Flu-like symptoms
• Pain
• Gastrointestinal problems
• Weight changes
• Hair loss
• Blood clotting issues
• Skin changes
• Kidney and bladder problems
• Anemia
• Infections

Respiratory Diseases[23]

There are many types of respiratory diseases, just to name a few: Asthma, chronic obstructive pulmonary disease (COPD), Emphysema, lung cancer, chronic bronchitis.

Asthma[23]

Occurs when the body's airways are sensitive to allergens and become inflamed. This inflammation can cause a painful and frightening asthma attack, which causes the airway muscles to tightened and narrow making it hard to breathe. Most people can manage their asthma very effectively with proper medication. However, asthma left unchecked can be fatal. On the average, three people die every day from an asthma attack. Symptoms of asthma include:

• Coughing
• A tight sensation in the chest
• Breathlessness

Older people are susceptible to asthma and should be on the lookout for symptoms, especially during the winter months. Asthma can worsen during and after a bout of the cold or flu.

COPD[23]

Is a chronic obstructive pulmonary disease that includes emphysema, chronic bronchitis that causes the flow of air in and out of the lungs to decrease. It affects millions of Americans and is the third -leading cause of death disease-related death in the USA.

Lung Cancer[23]

Is a disease of older persons. The incidence rates rise steeply around 45-49 years and peak in the85-89 age group for males and 80-84 years age group for females. The median age of diagnosis in the USA is 70 years and 68 percent of the patients diagnosed after 65 years of age.

According to the American Lung Association, lung cancer is the most common cancer worldwide, accounting for 21 new cases during 2018. According to the National Institutes of Health, men are more susceptible to this disease than women. However, the incidence has dropped 36 percent in men over the past 42 years, while it has risen 84 percent for women. Black men and women are more likely to develop and die from lung cancer than any other racial or ethnic group. There are two key types of lung cancer:

Non-small Cell Lung Cancer (NSCLC)[23], which is the most common—accounting for 80-85 percent of the lung cancers.

Small-cell Lung cancer (SCLC). SCLC grows and spreads more quickly than NSCLS. There are two types of SCLC:

• *Small-cell carcinoma* is a very aggressive form of cancer and requires immediate treatment.

• *Combined-small-cell carcinoma*

Kardiac Monitor

Many elderly people take their health very seriously; those with heart disease are concerned with strokes. They have portable EKG Kardia Mobile 6L monitors, which can display bradycardia (Slow heart beat), normal

12

rhythm, or tachycardia (Fast heart beat), which is a signal that they are at risk of developing a stroke—which occurs to over 800,000 Americans every year. Be sure that you understand what you need to do. Here are the symptoms:

• Numbness or weakness in the Face.
• Confusion or trouble speaking or understanding speech.
• Trouble seeing in one or both eyes.
• Trouble walking, dizziness, or problem with balance.
• Severe headache with no known cause.

Cognitive Impairment Disorders (CID)[23]:

These are disorders which involve cognitive changes of aging and fully developed symptoms of mild-cognitive impairment (MCI), dementia, Alzheimer's disease (AD). Most degenerative conditions are characterized by insidious onset and gradually progressive decline. MCI is an intermediate state between normal cognition and dementia, which generally progresses to more serious loss of memory. Because the brain of the elderly person processes the information more slowly compared to a healthy adult, communicate with a slower pace and more distinctly; face your older clients by facing them so they can read your lips, check for understanding and repeat the message if necessary.

Cardiovascular Diseases[23]

Cardiovascular diseases are the second most common cause of acquired cognitive impairment. Vascular cognitive impairment includes heredity vascular dementias, post-stroke dementia, multi-infarct dementia, subcortical ischemic vascular disease and dementia, and MCI. Aging is a dominant factor in acquiring CID. When coaching these elderly students, there are several things that the coach needs to be aware of:

• Obtain a full understanding of the student's Cognitive, Affective, and Physical condition before you develop the lesson plan.
• Ask the student what they want to accomplish.
• Speak at a much slower pace so the student can understand you.
• Demonstrate your drills at a slower pace. Ask the elderly if she/he needs to rest.

13

- Repeat your comments and demonstrations repeatedly, and the same way each time.
- Do frequent communication about the status of the individual when doing a task.
- Use frequent breaks to have the senior repeat what he/she are learning.
- Gather information from the senior student's feedback to see if you must revamp your lesson plans.
- Have a lot of patience.
- Give a lot of positive reinforcement.
- Do not use the same lessons for all elderly persons, instead develop special tailored lessons for each individual.

Physical Impairment Disorders (PID)[23]

Acquired brain injuries result in many types of physical disabilities[23] such as epilepsy, cerebral palsy, cystic fibrosis, multiple sclerosis, spina bifida, Prader-Willi Syndrome. This category of symptoms affects a person's mobility, physical capacity, stamina, or dexterity, hearing and visual impairments. These conditions usually occur after birth as a result of damage to the brain through accidents, strokes, tumors. This can include brain, or spinal cord injuries, multiple sclerosis, cerebral palsy, respiratory disorders, epilepsy, visual and hearing impairments, and more. Many veterans have amputations of the limbs and mental disorders, which make coaching even more difficult.

The physical disability can also be hereditary or congenital where the person has been born with a physical disability. Besides the loss of motor control, there is depression and loss of self-esteem.

As a coach what can you do on the ski slope? You should adhere to the following:

- Obtain a full understanding of the student's condition.
- Ask the student what they want to accomplish.
- Be sure to use the correct ski tools to facilitate the proper movements.
- Do frequent communication about the status of the individual when doinga task. Seniors especially want to always know their progress status.
- Pace your lesson at a pace that the disabled senior can handle.
- You may have to take frequent breaks.

• Gather information from the older person's feedback to see if you must
• Revamp your lesson plans.
• Give a lot of positive reinforcements.
• Have a lot of patience.

Attention-Deficit Disorders (ADD)[23]

Attention-deficit Disorder[23] is a term commonly used to describe a neurological condition with symptoms of inattention, distractibility, and poor working memory. This dysfunction is predominantly an inattentive syndrome. The hallmark of symptoms include:
• Poor working memory
• Inattention
• Distractibility
• Poor executive function
This group of elderly require a lot of patience and skills to control their behavior. You may want to ask their friends or relatives for suggestion on what works. Follow the KISS principle: Keep it Simple. As I often tell the coaches when I teach a clinic, *"Be Brief, Be Quick, Be Gone."* Stay away from loud noises like the roaring snow guns, crowds of people, theme parks.

Attention-Deficit Hyperactive-Disorders (ADHD)[23]

ADD and ADHD[23] are not the same disorder. A person with ADD often lack the hyperactivity component that is a prominent symptom with this disorder. The disorder can be neurological or psychological disorder. There are at least three major different types of ADHD.
1. Impulsive-hyperactive ADHD, which includes forgetfulness and poor focus, organization, and listening skills.

• Fidgeting
• Squirming
• Getting up often when seated
• Running or climbing at inappropriate times
• Having trouble playing quietly
• Talking too much
• Talking out of turn or blurting out

- Interrupting
- Often "on the go" as if driven by a motor

2. Inattentive ADHD, which includes distracted, having poor concentration and organizational skills.

- Not paying attention to detail
- Making careless mistakes
- Failing to pay attention and keep on task
- Not listening
- Being unable to follow or understand instructions
- Avoiding tasks, the involve effort
- Being distracted
- Being forgetful
- Losing things that are needed to complete the task

3. Combined ADHD, which is the most common type; these elderly students never seem to slow down. This includes symptoms from both Impulsive and Inattentive ADHD.

The same discussion stated for the ADD students, applies here for the ADHD seniors. An authoritative-management style seems to work best for this group of students. If things really get out of hand; you may have to have a "Time Out" session.

Having a bucket-load of patience will be required for these special students.

Autism-Syndrome Disorder (ASD)[23]

Autism[23] is a spectrum of neurological development classified as a type of developmental disability that occurs in one percent of the individuals worldwide.

Everyone with autism is unique, and there is no one specific way the condition is presented. Individuals on the autistic spectrum typically experience difficulties with social communication and interaction with people. They may also exhibit restricted, repetitive patterns of behavior, interests, or activities. Symptoms are typically recognized between one- and two-years of age in boys. ASD is more than four times more common among boys than among girls. About one in six (77 percent) children (Aged 3-

16

17years) were diagnosed with a developmental disability during a study period of 2009-2017. Based on these statistics, you can anticipate a rise in this disorder in seniors down the road. These include ASD, ADD/ADHD, blindness, cerebral palsy, among others. The problem seems to be worsening. In a study with four-year-old's, ASD gradually increased between 2010 and 2014. Depression and suicide are common in adult ASD, so there is little information on ASD in seniors. The term spectrum refers to the variation in the type and severity of the symptoms. Those in the mild range are typically able to function independently, with some difficulties in their daily lives. Those with moderate to severe symptoms may require more substantial support. Long-term problems may include:

• Difficulties in daily living
• Managing schedules
• Hypersensitivities to sound, light, etc.
• Creating and keeping relationships
• Inducing self-injuries; a study on eight-year-old children with ASD, had 28 percent of the participants that did self-injury to themselves (Headbanging, arm-biting, skin-scratching, hair-pulling, eye poking), making this a very common problem.

Some of the common symptoms of ASD include:

• Unresponsive to others
• Minimal eye contact
• Does not share interest with others
• Does not pretend in play
• Shows little interest in peers
• Has trouble understanding other people's feelings or talking about their own feelings
• Have restricted or repetitive behaviors or interests
• Lining up in line for the chairlifts or other scenarios and they can get upset when the order is changed
• Repeats words or phrases over and over
• Plays with toys the same way every time
• Is focused on parts of objects
• Gets upset by minor changes

- Has obsessive interests
- Must follow certain routines
- Flaps hands, rocks body, or spins self in circles
- Has unusual reactions to the way things sound, smell, taste, look or feel
- Delayed language skills
- Delayed movement skills
- Delayed cognitive or learning skills
- Hyperactive, impulsive, and/or inattentive behavior
- Unusual eating sleeping habits
- Unusual mood or emotional reactions
- Anxiety, stress, or excessive worry
- Lack of fear or more fear than expected

Asperger's Syndrome (AS)[23]

Asperger's syndrome[23] is a neurological disorder that is a mild form of ASD. As a (ASD) coach, you will more than likely be assigned to teach AS rather than ASD. Asperger's Syndrome is often considered a high functioning form of ASD because adults with the disorder can develop cognitive functions that match or exceed those of healthy adults. However, their skills may be impaired by their ability to interact with others. A recent study demonstrated that during adolescence and young adulthood, nearly 40 percent spent little or no time with friends. These characteristics perpetuate itself into adulthood and senior-hood.

Asperger's typically do not experience speech and language delays due to the above-average cognitive skills. The most common symptom is impaired social development. Adults with AS focus obsessively on specific and often unusual topics. Therefore, many individuals with this disorder can become experts on certain topics. However, they have been described as socially awkward and lacking social maturity. Here are some facts about AS:

• *Sensory issues*

They are usually hyper-sensitive to bright light, loud noises, and certain clothing fabric. For example, a buzzing noise that goes unnoticed by other individuals may be bothersome to an AS person. Lights that are blinking, bright or flashing are common instigators. The sensation of certain fabric against their skin can be irritating and distracting, which can cause distress.

• *Emotional challenges*

Children with AS may have issues with social development. For instance, they may lack empathy due to delays in social and emotional development. They may also struggle to understand nonverbal communication and nonliteral phrases, such as facial expressions. Anxiety and anger management in social situations can be a challenge for ski instructors. Many times, an AS person will express distress through emotions that do not match the situation—something that is a mild annoyance to most adults can be deeply upsetting and frustrating to seniors.

• *Social challenges*

Just as senior citizens with ASD, people with AS often prefer to play by themselves and they tend to be more self-focused. In other words, they focus more on themselves than on others in conversations and playing. Social cues such as body language and facial expression is usually missed. They can also miss the coach's hand motions (Such as 'come here', 'stop') making it seem that the individual is ignoring the senior citizen ski instructor or the elderly is being disobedient.

• *Behavior therapies*

Although AS elderly are different from other people, they should not be treated all that differently. They should be praised for their good deeds and skiing accomplishments. Likewise, they should be disciplined like any other children and given the same structure and routine. Seniors should be treated with more diplomacy and like the young folks, with the same structure and routine. Likewise, older folks face the same challenges and should be treated in a similar fashion.

As a coach, what should you do? Focus on the major issues, like do not look at your student in the eye, be careful of loud sounds (Snow guns running), keep the student's drills the same; do not make changes, do not touch the student, be patient, talk to his/her friends on how to deal with the elderly person. Gather information from your astute observations to see if you must revamp your lesson plans. Keep the tasks simple and short. Set realistic goals for this ASD elderly. Stay calm. Always, *"Expect the Unexpected."*

Down Syndrome (DS)[23]

These is a genetic disorder, where there is a chromosome abnormality, that is passed on by either parent.[23] There are over 200,000 babies born every with this disorder, causing intellectual disability, developmental delays, and physical appearance changes. The clinical features are as follows:

• Eyes are shaped like almonds.
• The shape of the face is flatter, especially the nose; the ears are smaller and may fold over a bit the top.
• Tongue tends to stick out of their mouth.
• They may have small hands, fingers, and feet.
• They may have low muscle tone and strength.
• They may have loose joints, making them very flexible.
• They may have a short height and neck.
• The head tends to be smaller.
• They may have mild to moderate cognitive capacities, their ability to think, reason, understand is compromised.
• Their social skills may be diminished.
• Behavioral problems may exist, such as not being able to pay attention well.
• They can be obsessive about some things.
• They seem to have a harder time to control their impulses.
• They have a harder time to manage their feelings when they get frustrated or stressed.
• They are more likely to have hearing losses, visual problems, heart and endocrine issues (Especially the thyroid gland).

What can you do as a ski instructor?

- Keep the teaching short and simple to minimize the frustrating circumstances or by introducing stressful tasks and drills. Follow the KISS principle.
- Keep the drills the same each time you practice a given task.
- Kids with this syndrome are very social and they love affection.
- Sometimes they will misbehave because of some underlying reason that you may have created.
- Provide lots of positive reinforcements to help build their self-esteem and self-confidence. Hugs, if permitted, will go a long way; pole taps, high fives, and fist bumps are alternative ways to provide positive reinforcements.
- Change your attitude and coaching approach if tasks or instructions fail; use the same ideas but modify the way you deliver the message.
- Rewards are important for all people, especially seniors with disabilities. For them it is a merit badge of honor. For the adults and seniors, I reward them with verbal positive comments.
- Pick your battles; is the behavior dangerous or just bothersome?
- Avoid power struggles by giving them choices or alternative pathways(Stepping-stones) to accomplish the same objectives.
- Make the harder tasks and drills more fun and less complicated to do.
- Make it less challenging and offer games to have fun and take away the stigma that it is too difficult to do. With dangerous behaviors, the student needs more structure and boundaries.
- Have "time out" periods to cool off the behavior issues.
- Be sure to communicate with the older student's friends. Ask for tips on what works and don't work.
- Have patients. Know your skills with these adaptive older folks.

The morale of the story is, follow the *Triple-A Rule*:

- Be **A**ware
- Be **A**lert
- Be **A**ttentive

Visually Impaired Disorder (VID)[23]

There are about 12.2 percent of the Seniors in the USA that have a diagnosed eye and vision disorder.

Here are some important facts about older folks with VID:

1. 15.2 percent of adults over 75 years are blind.
2. Cognitive disability had a greater influence on prevalence and kind of emotional and behavioral problems in seniors with visual impairment, such as age-related macular degeneration, glaucoma, cataract, and diabetic retinopathy.
3. Social skills are compromised in children and adults with VID.
4. Proprioception is compromised in the VID person; thus, space awareness around the child, adult, and elderly. is an issue. The coach's eyes will have to be the VID person's eyes.
5. Lazy eye (Amblyopia) is found in two percent of young children, which makes it the most common vision loss issues. This condition is due to abnormal development of the neural connection between the brain and the eye muscles during early childhood and unless corrected, persists into adulthood and into senior-hood.
6. The common types of VID include loss of central vision, which creates ablur or blind spot, but with intact peripheral vision, loss of peripheral vision, blurred vision, general hazed vision, extreme light sensitivity, and night blindness.
7. CVI or cortical/cerebral visual impairment is the leading cause of modern-day blindness in children, adults and the senior citizens.
8. Retinitis Pigmentosa, Macular Degeneration and Retinopathy of Prematurity make up the four most common cause of blindness in children and adults.
9. Some of the clinical signs of VID include:

• Not able to see objects at a distance
• Having trouble reading
• Not able to focus on objects or follow them. They may often squint and rub their eyes a lot or have chronic eye redness or sensitivity to light.

10. VID students may bump into things often.
11. Be especially careful if your elderly student is taking a lesson at night.

What can you do as a ski coach?
- Be physically close to your student
- Communicate a lot
- Your eyes will be their eyes
- Know about assistive devices, technology, and other learning aids
- Use ski slopes with minimal obstacles
- Have a game plan to include fun games and mechanics of movements to get the skis to respond
- Be sure the student is wearing a brightly colored vest that indicates that she/he is VID or blind so the skiing public is aware • VID students may need a ski harness for safety

Photo 3. A VID senior is wearing a bright-colored vest to warn the public is aware to stay clear and give a lot of space.

Hearing-Impaired Disorders (HID)[23]

Hearing-impaired disorders[23] is relatively common among children, adults and especially seniors. Approximately 1.9 percent of children have trouble hearing, and permanent hearing loss is found in more than 1 out of every 1000 children. About 2 percent of adults aged 45-54 have disabling hearing loss. Age is the strongest predictor of hearing loss among adults with men having twice as likely as women to have hearing loss. There are over 165 million people over 65 years with disabling hearing loss—33 percent of the world's population. Some facts about HID:

- Congenital, infections, physical accidents are common causes of hearing loss or impairments.
- Hearing loss can be acquired through Rubella, syphilis, herpes, jaundice, toxoplasmosis.
- Meningitis, sepsis, certain medications (Some antibiotics, diuretics).
- Head injuries, chronic middle-ear infections, some neurologic disorders (Hunter's syndrome, neurofibromatosis), exposure to high levels of noise for prolong periods.
- If senior clients do not respond to sounds, have difficulty talking, or are slow starting to talk, their hearing may be impaired.
- Untreated HID can impede an adult's verbal, social, and emotional development.
- Among adults aged 70 and older with hearing loss, could benefit from hearing aids, but fewer than 30 percent has ever used them. Hearing aids have made great progress and may be helpful; but today's technology still has not conquered the interference of surrounding background noise, which can be very disturbing.
- Try to have the HID student observe your face so they can read your lips.

How to recognize HID?

- Seniors appear to be ignoring people who are talking to them—some but not all the time.
- Elders can talk and hear well at home but not elsewhere because of the interferences from surrounding background noise. As many advancements the technology has created, they have still not resolved the background noise; it is still bothersome and irritating.

What can you do as a ski coach?

24

- Speak slowly and more distinctly.
- Speak with greater vocal volume, short of yelling which may scare the person, or the adult may think that you are trying to discipline him\her.
- Try to stand directly in front of the student so the person can read your lips.
- If the person is wearing a hearing aid, check to see if there is enough charge in the battery, especially in sub-zero weather. The severe wind may interfere with hearing because the wind will force the voice away from the hearing aid and will cause distraction due to the background noise.
- Try to stay away from the snow guns when they are making snow and large crowds of people.
- Communicate with the HID senior client to gain some tips on how to deal with the senior's hearing issues on the ski slopes.

Speech Impairment Disorders (SID)[23]

Speech impairment disorder[23] are disorders of speech sounds, fluency, or voice that interfere with communication. It may include articulation disorder, characterized by omissions or distortions of speech sounds, a fluency disorder, characterized by atypical flow, rhythm, and/or repetition of sounds or stuttering, or voice disorder, characterized by abnormal pitch, volume, resonance, vocal quality, or duration. About 7.7 percent of USA children between ages 3-17 have a disorder related to voice, speech, language, or swallowing. Likewise, adults and seniors have about 5% SID.

Here are some facts of SID in people:
- Roughly 7.5 million adults in the U.S. have trouble using their voice.
- About three million children stutter. It affects individuals of all ages but occurs most frequently in young children between the ages of 2 and 6, and they outgrow that if they attend speech pathology school.
- This disorder occurs predominantly in boys, ranging 1.5 to 2.4 ratio boys to girls. Most adults outgrow stuttering. However, Seniors may begin to stutter again, often due to neurogenic reasons. Perhaps a stroke has altered areas of their brain that controls language processing and correct formulation of words or bumps that may have caused a concussion or other speech problems. They're other things such a brain trauma, epilepsy, drug abuse.
- The types of SID include Spasmodic Dysphonia (A voice disorder caused by involuntary movements of one or more muscles of the larynx or voice

box); Laryngeal Papillomatosis (Caused by tumors that grow inside the voice box, vocal cords, or the air passages leading from the noise into the lungs. It is caused by HPV virus, which is found between 60 and 80 percent in children, usually before the age of 3; cleft palate is the fourth most common birth defect, which affect 5 to 8 percent of children. Do not be surprise that seniors are affected by the same disorder.

- The most common SID is stuttering and lisp.
- A child with SID delay is likely to have difficulty following instructions, especially if the instructions are only given orally and they contain multiple words and/or steps. An adult with SID will have the same difficulties.
- A student with SID may have difficulty learning how to read and spell.

What are some of the causes of SID?

- Brain damage due to head trauma
- Throat muscle weakness
- Damage to the vocal cords
- Degenerative diseases, such as Huntington's disease, Parkinson's disease, or amyotrophic lateral sclerosis
- Dementia
- Cancer that affected the mouth or throat
- Autism
- Down's syndrome

What can you do as a ski coach?

- Communicate with your hands more — remember, "A picture is Worth More than A Thousand Words;" you can always draw pictures in the snow.
- Speak slowly and more distinctly.
- You may need to speak with greater vocal volume, short of yelling which may scare some adults or elderly persons, or the person may think that you are trying to discipline him/her.
- Try to stand directly in front of the student so the child can read your lips.
- Try to stay away from the snow guns when they are making snow.
- Communicate with the seniors to gain some tips on how to deal with the mon the ski slopes.

Osteoporosis[23]

This is a bone disease with less bone density and bone strength. Fracture of the bone is common because of the frail nature of the bones. Osteoporosis is common in women undergoing menopause because estrogen helps with the bone remodeling process. Some of the risk factors associated with this disease are the following:

• It is more common in women, especially in postmenopausal women.
• Aging process creates more complicated ailments as you get older your risk increases.
• Body size matters: small, thin women are at a greater risk.
• Asian and white women have the highest risk.
• Genetics play a role if there is a family history.
• Lack of exercise will weaken bones.
• Poor diet plays a role; lack of calcium and vitamin D plays a role.
• Some medications may increase the risk.
• Smoking may increase the risk.
• Excessive alcohol intake can cause bone loss.
• Lack of sunshine or vitamin D and calcium intake may cause bone loss.

If the senior client has begun treatment for osteoporosis, do low-impact drills to protect the bones for the client.

Diseases of the Mind[23]

This category of diseases covers a large gamut of cognitive dysfunctions, such as mild-cognitive impairment (MCI), dementia, and Alzheimer's disease (AD), which is ranked 6th leading cause of death in the elderly in the USA. Alzheimer's disease is the most common cause of MCI, accounting for 34-75 percent of all patients. MCI is a condition in which people have memory or other thinking problems greater than normal for their age and education, but their symptoms are not as severe as those seen in individuals AD. The problems associated with MCI may also be caused by certain medications, cerebrovascular disease and other factors. The type of MCI with memory loss as the main symptom is called amnestic MCI. In another type, non-amnestic MCI, the main symptom is an impaired thinking skill other than memory loss, such as trouble planning and organizing or poor judgement.

What is dementia? It is a neurological brain degradation that affects memory loss. Cognitive decline, confusion in the evening hours, disorientation, inability to speak or understand languages, inability to recognize common things are common—making it more serious than MCI. There are also, mood swings, depression, jumbled speech, sleep disorder, falling. What is Alzheimer's disorder? People with AD cannot recall elementary things like where their home is located, cannot remember the simplest things, which make them repeat the same question over and over. Another huge challenge is organizing tasks, managing time, following chronological order, and lack of concentration.

Because short-term memory loss is an issue, as a coach, speak slowly and clearly; you may want to repeat yourself. Certainly, check for understanding by having the senior citizen repeat your instructions.

Depression[23]

This is a mental-health issue. Anxiety and depression often go hand in hand. Depression can sound like being in a bottomless hole, whereas anxiety can seem like a condition in which affected seniors are full of energy. For this reason, it seems counterintuitive that someone could experience them simultaneously. And yet, it is not only possible but also common. Depression is the leading cause of disability in America in teenagers and adults. The depression symptoms are:

- Overwhelming feeling of sadness
- Loss of interest and pleasure in most usual activities
- Decrease or increase in appetite
- Insomnia
- Psychomotor agitation or retardation
- Constant fatigue
- Recurrent thoughts of death and suicidal ideation with or without specific plans for committing suicide.
- Bipolar 1 and 2 are included in this depression group.

On the other hand, symptoms of anxiety disorders are the following:

- Pounding or racing heart
- Sweating or cold, clammy hands
- Feeling jumpy or restless

- Trembling, twitching, or shaking
- Having a hard time catching your breath
- Feeling a fullness in the throat or chest
- Feeling dizzy or lightheaded
- Having stomachaches or nausea
- Having problems falling asleep

Falls[1-3]

Each year, millions of older people—those 65 and older—fall. In fact, 25 percent fall each year, but less than half tell their doctors. Falling once doubles your chance of falling again. This is a serious disorder:
- About 20 percent of the falls cause a serious injury such as broken bones or head injuries.
- Each year, 3 million elderlies are treated in the ER for fall injuries.
- Over 800,000 patients a year are hospitalized because of a fall injury, most often because of a head injury or hip fracture (About 300,000).
- More than 95 percent of hip fractures are caused by falling; usually by falling sideways.
- Falls are the most common cause of traumatic brain injuries (TBI).
- Total cost for falls totaled more than $50 billion.
- Because the senior's legs are weak, they cannot get up on their own; the senior specialist coach can demonstrate how to use their one ski as a crutch to get up facing to the side of the hill.

Many falls do not cause injuries. But the one's that do cause injuries can make it hard for a person to get around, do everyday activities, or live on their own.

Some current statistics include:
- Falls can cause broken bones, like wrist, arm, ankle, and hip fractures.
- Falls can cause head injuries. Some can be very serious, especially if the person is taking certain medication (Like blood thinners for prevention of strokes) that will cause unstoppable bleeding.
- Senior individuals who fall does fewer physical activities are, thus, weaker and increases their chances of falling. Individuals with vision problems, foot issues, weak leg muscles, and on uneven terrain run the risk of falling. That is why it is required by law when you visit the doctor, they need to

ask, "have you fallen recently"? Most falls are caused by a combination of risk factors, the more the risk factors the person has, the greater the chances of falling.

• Falling on the snow is one of the greatest concerns of the elderly; be extremely careful with the seniors.

Pain, medications, side-effects[1-3]

Because pain is such a common complaint for people getting older, we need to be more diligent in recognizing and adapting our lesson plans to adjust for this issue. Seniors use alcohol and prescription pain medications (Opioids) to help relieve pain. Here are some facts on old folks taking opioids:

▶ At least 20 percent of the elderly have taken on the average, filled at least one outpatient out-patient opioid prescription, and 7.4 percent have obtained 7.1 percent 4 or more prescriptions during the year.

▶ Elderly adults who are poor (9.5 percent) or low income (11.3 percent) are more likely than middle income (6.8 percent), and high income (4.5 percent) older adults to obtain four or more opioid prescription fills during the year.

▶ An average annual total of 9.8 million of adults, or 25.3 percent of the 60 million senior adults in the USA in non-institutionalized population.

▶ Opioid prescriptions in the emergency department have increased over 50 percent between 2010-2015.

▶ Some common side-effects of opioids:
• Drowsiness
• Confusion
• Nausea
• Constipation
• Euphoria
• Slow breathing
• Addiction

▶ How does the opioid crisis affect you as a ski coach?

When seniors use opioids on a regular base for pain, they face a special set of challenges because of their generally reduced metabolism, excretion, and physical reserves. Be aware that as the seniors age, the opioid acts more potently, causing more severe side effects, such as MCI, respiratory depression, effects on endocrine system, and CVD.

Feet & Ankle Swelling

A very common medical condition is often overlooked in the elderly. About 70 percent of the older folks have these medical conditions. Congestive
Heart Failure (CHF) is the most common cause of edema. This also called "lower extremity edema" because the return of the blood from the veins tend to "leak" out of the veins to the outside of the blood vessels to the interstitial spaces of the body causing swelling or edema. To help prevent this condition, you can recommend that they reduce their salt intake, exercise the calf muscles, get frequent leg massages, and eat a healthier diet with more fruits and vegetables. This swelling causes the seniors to not tighten their boot buckles enough; this makes the person to not be stable in the boots, which can cause more frequent falling when skiing.

Fatigue

This condition is one of the most underestimated and unrecognized physical condition of the elderly person that will affect their skiing outcome:
▶ Loss of lean body mass — The amount of muscle loss (Sarcopenia) in a senior person can be significant. After 50 years of age, sarcopenia increases to one to two percent yearly. This naturally occurring disorder affects as much as 50 percent of the senior persons in their 80s. Because people are living longer these days, sarcopenia is an increasingly prominent issue, affecting the health, well-being, and quality of life of the older population. To help overcome this process, diets with good quality proteins will help; eggs have the correct balance of the eight essential amino acids that can help build muscle mass. These are the symptoms of sarcopenia:

• Being tired and exhausted
• Falling
• Muscle weakness

- Slow walking speed
- Self-reported muscle wasting
- Difficulty performing normal daily activities

▶ Being overweight or obese — Elderly Americans are being confronted with this epidemic health condition as the years move on—30 percent of men and women presently — and will continue to grow with time. More of this topic can be found under *Obesity* in chapter 3. Fatigue sets in quickly because of all the extra weight an elderly person is carrying, in addition to loss of lean-muscle mass. This is the case of the person eating too many of mom's favorite apple pies; the daily caloric intake exceeds the caloric output.

▶ Physical conditioning & muscle strength — According to surveys on the senior citizens, only 50 percent continue to be active in later life. The other half will struggle on the ski hill at the end of the ski lesson. Physical fitness is a state of health and well-being and, more specifically, the ability to perform aspects of sports, occupations, and daily activities. Physical fitness is generally achieved through proper nutrition, moderate-vigorous physical exercise, and sufficient rest along with a formal recovery plan. There are five components of physical fitness:

- Cardiovascular endurance
- Muscular strength
- Muscular endurance
- Flexibility
- Body composition

What can a senior citizen ski instructor do?

I had Kris Quinn as my senior citizen examiner. Fortunately, she was an astute and compassionate examiner and instructor. Towards the end of the day, she noticed that I, at age 79 ½ years, was getting tired. She made the discussions less lengthy with less hard-impact drills. After our lunch--and frequent restroom breaks--she carried my skis to the area where we were supposed to meet as a group on the terrain. This is a true example of an outstanding senior citizen instructor. All the truck-load of money could not buy that kind of compassion and caring!

Chapter 4

The American Teaching System

The teaching style for the Seniors, is based on the American Teaching System (ATS)[1] for adults with modifications. This teaching guidelines will provide consistency on how we teach throughout America. ATS is a progression oriented, outcome based and student-centered teaching blueprint.

Principles and Philosophies
▶ Student Centered — The lesson topics are based on the student's needs
▶ Outcome Based — There is an outcome to every lesson
▶ Experiential — Individuals learn by doing it and not just by hearing, also known as learning by self-discovery
▶ Learning-Partnership Based — The child and instructor develop the lesson components together
▶ Guest-Service Driven — Students are the guests; they deserve to be taught by a specialized coach trained in this specialty

Components
1. Teaching Model
• Instructor Profile — Senior Teaching Model
• Student Profile — Background and motivation, learning preferences, attitude and other CAP issues

The teaching style for the seniors, is based on the American Teaching System (ATS) for adults with modifications. This teaching guidelines will provide consistency on how we teach throughout America. ATS is a progression oriented, outcome based and student-centered teaching blueprint.

1. Be aware of The Senior Specialist Teaching/Learning Cycle[21] that centers on three core characteristics:

- *Pacing* — to make the class lessons as enjoyable as possible, make the social experience a real value-added change without taxing the stamina and endurance of the client. Having fun, taking breaks, enjoying the scenery, and discussing topics of choices are all critical.

- *Relationships* — the social aspect is critical to the senior person. Developing a senior student profile, creating connections by demonstrating a genuine interest in the client, and to ensure that the client enjoyed the mountain experience to constantly check for understanding.

- *Low-impact drills and exercises* — are encouraged (e.g., Stacking of the body over the feet) to reduce the amount of muscular stress required to maintain balance[12, 18] and still accomplish the desired goals. Also, the body movements should be continuous and flowing[21].

2. Alpine Five Fundamentals of Skiing Model — Direct pressure to the outside ski, pressure control from ski to ski, be balanced over the downhill ski, adjusting pressure on the skis[18]

3. Alpine Skiing/Snowboarding Model[4-7, 18, 25]

4. Alpine Skiing Skills Concept Model—edging-, pressure-, and rotary control, plus balance[18]

5. Service model

- Introduction—Meet and greet everyone session
- Effective communication—Adapt to the student's style of talking (Pace, tone, volume, speech pattern)

A Student-Coach partnership[18, 25] must develop through constant and open communication for success to develop with your senior's lessons. The information provided by the student must provide complete and transparent information to the ski instructor so he/she can know the exact and complete profile of your student to create a specific lesson plan tailored to the needs of your elderly student with or without handicaps. In addition, you need to always be prepared--*expect the unexpected.*

A key part of your senior's lesson plan will revolve around the PSIA CAP Model.[4-7, 18, 25] Every elderly person declines at a different rate at a given age, and a senior specialist coach, needs to know the different developmental stages of the cognitive, motional/social, and physical developmental to create *realistic*[7, 12, 25] goals, and not *ideal*[7, 12,25] goals that the person cannot achieve. A self-defeated person is always feels unsuccessful and unhappy. Be mindful that everyone wants to be acknowledged that they did a great job. The child seeks accolades so his/her parent can complement the accomplishments that were achieved. That is one of the rewards that we all seek. So, do give a lot of hi-fives on the slope. This is also a motivational factor that will stimulate the senior to try harder, work harder. In this regard, whenever a coach gives feedback, it should always be *positive*, never negative because it will affect his/her self-esteem.

When doing lesson plans, use the PSIA CAP Model,[1-7, 18, 25] which revolves around the elderly's **C**ognitive, **A**ffective, and **P**hysical developmental stages.

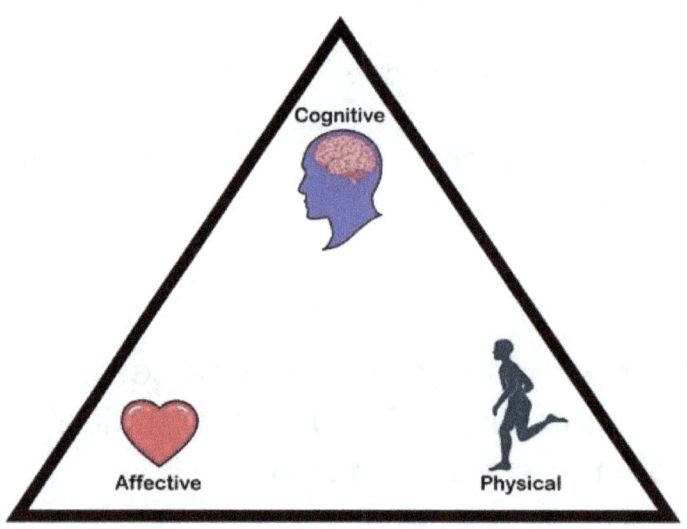

Figure 2. The PSIA CAP Model: Cognitive, Affective, and Physical Developments.

Understanding this model, will aid you in recognizing the way they think, their emotion/social behaviors, and physical limits. This information will greatly help you with planning a successful lesson. The coach can adjust the lesson plans based on the information gathered and the *learning style* of the special needs senior citizen:

Learning Styles[12, 18, 25]

People learn with different *Learning Styles*[12, 18, 25] According to psychologists, there are five Elements of Learning: physiological, environmental, sociological, physiological, and emotional. There are many learning styles (Verbal, visual, musical/auditory, physical/kinesthetic, combination, solitary, social, logical/mathematical). However, it can be simplified and boiled down to the *VAK Model*[25] (See figure 4). It should be emphasized that the different styles of learning may not translate to learning the material: it simply means, according to many published reports, students prefer to receive information for processing in a specific way (e.g., Visually, or hearing the message, or feeling how to do a task).

The primary and secondary learning styles will vary, depending on the activity involved. The bottom line is, don't get too hung up on just learning styles because people learn by various methods depending on the circumstances. It is much better to think of a student having a toolbox that contains ways to think, memorize, and employ a task. However, there are many learning specialists that recommend that you hold on to a framework of the different learning styles so you can provide a rich, varied presentation when you present a new movement, activity, or skill. Do acknowledge the importance of the *Senior Specialist learning Partnership Requirements Cycle*[21] (See figure 3).

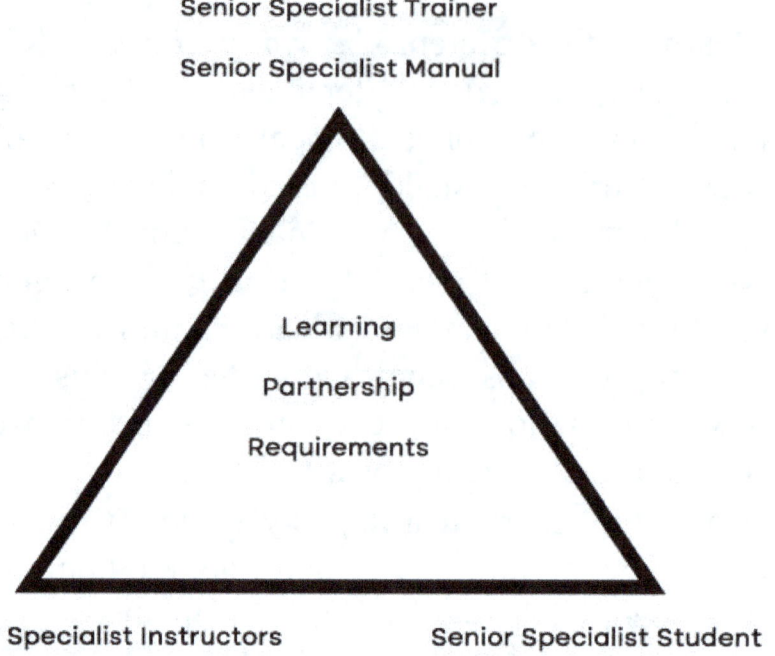

Senior Specialist Trainer

Senior Specialist Manual

Learning

Partnership

Requirements

Senior Specialist Instructors   Senior Specialist Student

Figure 3. Senior Specialist Learning Partnership Requirments[21]

Understand the *VAK Model*[18, 25] when creating your lesson plans: the three pathways by which a signal gets to the brain. (See figure 4).

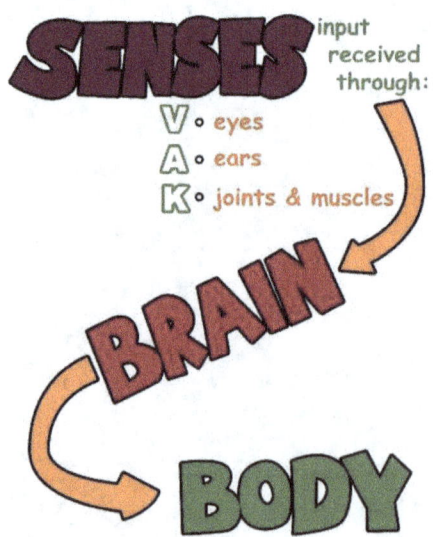

Figure 4. *VAK Model: A learning style*[18, 25]

Visual

These individuals learn best when charts, graphics, images, drawings, pictures, and photographs are used instead of words. They store information in the brain as a picture and need to watch and mimic movements. They look for good demonstrations so they can copy the coach's body movements.

Auditory

These individuals like spoken words, prefer lectures and discussions over pictures. They store information as a running commentary and need to know the *how* and *why*. These individuals tend to like to listen to music, sing, and listen to the radio.

Kinesthetic

These individuals like tactile processes; they prefer to create concrete personal experiences and like to process the information by recreating and practicing. They learn best by doing activities to experience how it feels. Do ask your students, "What did you feel when doing that movement?" With this *type of learners*, the **results** are:
• I Hear, but I forget…
• I See, and I remember…
• I Do, and I understand…

Feeler

These types of students need to feel the movement and activity that they are doing. So, as a senior specialist coach, you need to help them with w*hat*, w*here*, *how,* w*hen* to feel the movements. Remember, kinesthetic implies feeling *outside* the body; proprioceptive means feeling *within* the body.

Watcher

These types of students are visual learners and want to see how you do it (Do accurate and precise demonstrations. These visual learners target their attention to specific areas (What body parts move, how the skis respond to the movements) and prefer views from different angles. Drawing in the snow, using your hands, or using metaphors will often provide the necessary picture that they need for their brain to process. Your demonstrations need to be spot on! The same applies on what we discussed above under Visual in the VAK Model.

Thinker

These types of students ask many *how and why* questions and learn best by using cognitive abilities. They want details; so, you should provide a rational as to *Why, How, When, and Where* to teach a movement. They prefer a direct dialogue with you to do a verbal and/or visual discussion with them. Depending on their age, they can generally deal with abstract concepts. While keeping the instructions simple, do ask your students, "Why are we doing that drill or if I do this body movement incorrectly, What are the effects on the skis?"

Doer

These types of students want the big picture and what is necessary; they will attempt to do self-discovery on how to do it, with proper guidance from you. They will do a lot of experimentation and discover by trial and error for the desired outcome. These students usually want to be first to go. It should be stated that *intrinsic feedback* should be a supplement to the learning styles. Intrinsic feedback is the student's inner voice. In addition to giving extrinsic feedback, instructors need to ask students to share what they think and feel about what they are doing. For example, the student did a task and the coach said, *"Good job or that was awesome."*

A Student-Coach partnership[18, 25] must develop through constant and open communication for success to develop with your student's lessons. A key part of your senior citizen's lesson plan will revolve around the PSIA CAP Model.[1-7,18, 25] Every senior person age at a different rate at a given age, and the senior coach needs to know the different aging process of the cognitive, motional/social, and physical developmental to create *realistic*[7, 12, 25] goals, and not *ideal*[7, 12, 25] goals that the senior person cannot achieve.

A self-defeated to be person is always feels unsuccessful and unhappy. Be mindful that everyone wants acknowledged as they did a great job. The child seeks accolades so his/her friends and members of the family and relatives can complement the stimulate the senior citizen to try harder, work harder. In this regard, whenever a coach accomplishment that were achieved. That is one of the rewards that we all seek. So, do give a lot of hifives on the slope. This is also a motivational factor that will gives feedback, it should always be *positive*, never negative because it will affect his/her self-esteem. When doing lesson plans, use the PSIA CAP Model[4.]

[7,18,25] which revolves around the person's **C**ognitive, **A**ffective, and **P**hysical developmental stages.

Understanding this model, will aid you in recognizing the way they think, their emotion/social behaviors, and physical limits. This information will greatly help you with planning a successful lesson. The coach can adjust the lesson plans based on the information gathered and the *learning style* of the special needs child.

Chapter 5

Setting Realistic Goals

Student's Profile[18, 25]

By evaluating the student's ability to learn, we will be in a better position to develop a meaningful learning experience and teach the *Whole Person*. Be mindful that your lesson plan should be Student Centered.

When planning your lesson plan, consider the senior PSIA CAP *Model*[4-7, 18, 21, 25] (See figure 2). The PSIA *CAP Mode* can be very helpful when creating your lesson plan. Pay particular attention to the early phase of your meeting with your student. Try to analyze the student's profile for better understanding of a student's expectation and what they'll be able to accomplish on the hill; also, it provides a foundation for better lesson planning. This important topic is extensively covered in chapter 9. ***Cognitive*** Cognitive growth or decline involves an individual's ability to process information obtained through experiences. As a person ages, the nerve conduction speed slows down. Their brain processing speed slows down. Thus, you may need a couple of ounces of patience when coaching a 70- or 90-year-old student. It is their point of view based on their observation and thinking process.

How you communicate with the elders depends on their Cognitive development:

• How they process the information in their brain
• How they express themselves
• How they reason or think

Affective

Affective growth involves the senior's sense of humor, self-identity, self-esteem, (How they associate and socialize with others, their ability to follow rules, moral values). Do not underestimate the importance of assessing the person's developmental stages to create a successful lesson plan.

Physical

Physical growth includes how seniors move; muscle and skeletal development (Motor control, balance, coordination, center of mass, large and small muscle movements and coordination). Being tall or small, skinny or over-weight, 50-years-old or 90-years-old student can be deceiving, when it comes to physical maturation and coordination. Even though 50 percent of the elderly do not participate in any organized physical activities, the other 50 percent do. Try to encourage the 50 percent who do not exercise to partake in some sort of regular activity to help with their muscle strength and coordination, endurance on the ski slopes, bone strength, and balance. The amount of time it takes your muscles to atrophy depends on your age, fitness level and cause of atrophy. If your muscle atrophy is due to disuse (Physiologic), the process takes two to three weeks. Generally, the atrophy involves muscle wasting (Loss of muscle mass) and amyotrophic lateral sclerosis (ALS), which is a progressive disease that affects the nerve cells throughout the body that die and stop functioning. Be especially careful about the senior's balance throughout the lesson.

As a senior specialist coach, you need to figure out your student's cognitive development. For example, communication with older adults can be a real challenge. Does an 85-year-old student know what you mean by a left turn or a right turn? Never assume that they do; many may not. Your senior client may have some sort of cognitive dysfunction. They may have dementia, MCI, autism, or brain tumor. Some seniors with cognitive disorders seem to know colors much better than verbal commands. So, why not place a red sticker on their right-hand glove and a green sticker on their left-hand glove? Now you can instruct them to make a green turn or a red turn. Avoid placing stickers on the toes of their boots because they tend to look down at the stickers, which will cause them to be out of balance—keep their chin up. I cannot stress enough that as a successful senior teacher, it is imperative that you must be *creative* and *imaginative*. Keep it *simple*, keep it *short*, and keep the instruction *clear and understandable* by checking how they perceived your instructions. Also, by make it *fun*. So, always: *"Be brief, Be brilliant, Be gone!"*

Everyone needs to be *motivated*. How do you motivate an older person to do something that they are not in the mood to do, fear of doing, or disinterested in doing? Your enthusiasm for the sport, your passion for coaching, and your commitment to *exceeding customer satisfaction* will go a long way. Depending on how it is received, I may do magic tricks,[15, 20] or if they are musically inclined, play the harmonica.[8]

To succeed you need to be creative and have an insightful imagination. Remember as a snow sport instructor, you're in the *entertainment* business.

You are there to create *fun* and *excitement!* It begins with their mental attitude, which can then motivate their behavior. Building trust and bonding will create a connection with your client. Without that it is uphill battle implementing your lesson plans.

For example, during my hour-and-a-half drive to the ski resorts from my home, I remind myself that, "It's *show time!*" This allows me to mentally prepare myself as to who I'll be that day. Am I to be a clown? a magician[15, 20]? a ventriloquist[23] with one of my dozens of puppets? What color and style hair wig should I wear? If you are gifted with a beautiful voice, serenade the elderly student while riding up the chairlift. If you have any musical talents, jam with them by playing the harmonica[8] or kazoo. We all spent a lot of time creating those a-ha moments over the years, perfecting these different activities. Use those priceless creative resources of yours to add to your *bag of tricks* to help formulate these memorable moments for our senior students. The profile of the student may lead me to have a discussion on gardening, golfing, fishing or whatever I can do to connect with the elderly. My goal is to obtain as much information in the student's profile so that I can set realistic goals and not idealistic goals.[12, 25]

Photo 4. A senior citizen smiling because he had a great time socializing with friends on the ski slopes.

Chapter 6

<u>The Importance of Bonding and Trust</u>

I cannot over-emphasize how critical it is for YOU, the coach, to establish a *bond* and *trust*[12, 25] with your senior student. The learning connection with your client requires a *student-coach partnership* for a successful learning process on the hill. My first clue on the importance of bonding and trust came when I got a new animal to respond to my command. Have you ever noticed that when you get a new pet (Or a newborn baby), they seldom gravitate to you immediately? You need to spend the quality time to bond and develop trust with the cat, dog, horse, rabbit, or baby; otherwise, it just won't happen! Over the years, I had four equine-loving students that had a deep passion for horse riding and wanted to learn skiing. I curiously communicated with them and did a lot of research on horse training. You know, there are a lot of similarities with training people how to ski and training them how to ride a horse. Besides, seniors love hearing these types of stories; remember, seniors love to be entertained and socialize. For example,

1. You cannot ride a horse before developing a relationship; bonding and developing trust with one another is crucial. Likewise, a ski instructor that does not bond and develop trust with a ski student, will have difficulties with executing his/her ski lessons.

2. The bonding needs to be reinforced frequently by verbal communications, with body gestures (Rubbing the nose, forehead, neck areas called a "horse handshake"), and rewards like offering carrots or apples; likewise, seniors need the same treatment by their coaches to maintain the bonding process.

3. Safety is first; wearing a helmet is primary along with a properly fitted riding boots. Adults should always wear a properly fitted helmet.

4. Going slow before you ride faster (Walk, trot, canter, gallop) is always suggested; likewise, skiing on safe and gentle terrain and slowly is required before going fast, and even racing.

5. Learning to ride in a balanced position in the saddle is required before learning other fundamental movements; likewise, in skiing, we want the

student to master balance throughout the turns on the hills of different steepness.

6. The rider is required to be in synchronization and alignment with the galloping horse's rhythm; just as a skier's core (Center of Mass) needs to be in alignment with his/her feet (Base of Support).

7. A horse does not want to be treated roughly or be too tightly controlled; neither does a student." I tell you this tidbit of information because it can make you a better ski coach. How?

You will be surprised, many of your seniors come from rural areas where they have many experiences with horses. They may be able to tell you a thing or two about horses. By being creative, your job is to develop a lesson plan that will unlock your students' interests, motivation, and excitement about wanting to learn everything about skiing. To find the key to the lock, you need to discover where the key is located by asking a lot of creative questions, like what kind of sports, movies, or hobbies do you have a passion for?

If I find horse-lovers in the class, I always develop a lesson plan around horse-riding training because the learning curve is faster for those students. Sometimes you may not have the time to connect with the parent and child because of special circumstances, such as having group lessons, especially when the lessons consist of six or more students. However, you should adapt these concepts to *group* lessons whenever circumstances allow it. This manual primarily refers to *private* lessons. I'll start with the multiple ways that you can bond and develop trust with your students.

Photo 5. The 73 year-old horse trainer had a great time because his coach taught him the horse-riding training way how to ski and he connected right away and did super well because he lives on a horse farm and raises horses.

Chapter 7

Teaching The Skiing Concept Model and The Five Fundamentals of Skiing Model

Skills Concept and Five Fundamentals of Skiing Models[25]

Like any sport, skiing requires the development of specific skills. When creating the lesson plan with a goal, you need to be aware of the *Skills Concept Model,*[25] which evolved into the *Five Fundamentals of Skiing Model*[25] during 2018 This includes:

• Direct pressure to the outside ski and pressure control from ski-to-ski

• Edging control, ankles with Inclination and angulation

• Keeping the COM over the BOS

• Control the skis rotation with leg rotation

• Regulating the pressure created by ski/snow interaction.

As each skill develops, there are common body movements that exhibit themselves in skiers from the PSIA Level 1 through Level 9 (1, 2, 3 = Beginner; 4, 5, 6 = Intermediate; 7, 8 = Advanced; 9 = Expert). It is our job as instructors/ coaches to evaluate and isolate specific ineffective skills to help our students practice and correct them. Effective movement patterns are often quite different for children than for adults. It is especially important that we exercise patience and use repetition when teaching movements to senior citizens. Both the *Skills Concept Model and the Five*

Fundamentals of Skiing Model[25] comprise the central PSIA philosophy and the American Teaching System. The *Skills Concept* Model categorizes everything we can do that affects going to the right or to the left on a pair of skis. The Five Skiing Fundamentals filters the *Skills Concept Model* technical framework into what we see as mechanical imperatives for great skiing. Be mindful that Five Fundamentals of Skiing are easier to visualize and comprehend than the Skill Concept Model. I will briefly cover the Skills Concept Model[25] first, then the Five Fundamentals of Skiing

Model.[25] I will focus on the Five Fundamentals of Skiing, and cite references on the Skills that are discussed in greater detail elsewhere in this book. In addition, I will integrate the Skill Concept Model with the Five Fundamentals for skiing as much as possible. Your challenge as a coach is knowing how to integrate and blend the Skills Concept Model into the Five Fundamentals of Skiing Model.

Skills Concept Model[25] Edge Control

Is the ability to tip the ski onto its edge and adjust the angle between the base of the ski and the snow. The edge angle can be from flat to high edge, which has a significant impact on speed and directional change.

Effective edge control involves only using the amount of edge angle necessary to accurately affect the path of the ski through the arc of the turn. Skiers must move laterally to balance against the forces that act on the skis when they are tipped on edge.

There are two terms that are commonly used to describe body movements relative to edge-control skills: *angulation* and *inclination*.

Angulation

Refers to movements that create angles between body parts, (e.g., Hip angulation and knee angulation).

Inclination

Occurs when the skier deviates from a vertical position, which is a general term for any lateral movement toward the inside of the turn brought on by the forces caused during the change in direction of the skis. Other factors that cause inclination, include the edge angle used, the size and shape of the turn radius, the pitch of the hill, snow conditions, and speed. Edge control skills are discussed further in chapter 9.

Pressure Control

Pressure Control requires body movements to manipulate forces, which affect the action of the skis on the snow. With *fore/aft movements*, pressure can be applied to the entire length of the ski or specific parts of the ski, which requires a forward (Fore) or backward (Aft) adjustments between the skier's *Center of Mass*[25] (COM) and the child's *Base of Support*[25] (BOS). The COM is the central balance point of a person's body mass and the BOS is where the person's weight is distributed on the foot. A skier may move the COM fore or aft relative to the BOS by flexing the ankles more (Closing), or alternately by pulling both boots back, directly under the COM. Both of these body movements produce the same result by adjusting the pressure fore or aft to attain better balance. The most effective way to control the fore and aft COM is by flexing and extending the ankles. The ankles are an important part of the movements needs to alter the relationship of the BOS to the COM. *I repeat, the opening and closing of the ankles can move the COM forward and backward relative to the BOS.* In reality, it is a combination of the ankles, knees, hips and upper body to are required. The fore/aft pressure along the length of the ski can be controlled by moving the COM, BOS, or the combination of both. Making minute adjustments to these body segments is hard enough as an adult, let alone as a senior. Depending on where the older student falls physically in the PSIA CAP Model, these concepts may elude both physically and cognitively impaired older students. The challenge is finding creative ways to get elders to turn their skis (Rotational control), tip their skis (Edging and pressure control), and direct the pressure along the ski from foot to foot. The challenge is also, to manage changes in skis/snow interactions from to the bottom of the hill under different snow conditions and steepness. Another view of pressure control is *releasing* the pressure, instead of pushing, pressing, applying, stepping, flexing, squashing. Think of it as more like *lifting*. You can lift your inside knee into your chest, to transfer weight to your outside ski. This method allows you to absorb the energy from rebound (Retraction) and project it in the direction you intend to go. While pulling the inside ski up and back, you lift the outside of the hip and lead with the inside shoulder in (Keeping the strong inside half) to execute super slow, accurate, true parallel turns. When you are comfortable with this sequence of movements, you can increase the pace. These movements are very slight, subtle, deliberate, accurate smooth, like the flow of a great gymnast. You can also lift your toes while creating a well-balanced stance on your foot to allow more closing of the ankles (Dorsal-flex), if needed.

More information on pressure control[25] can be obtained in chapter 9.

Ski-to-Ski Movements

It is also necessary to control the pressure applied from ski-to-ski or footto-foot. During the change of direction, pressure is applied to the outside ski (Furthest away from the body's core), which causes the force to push on the skis for the change in direction. When linking the turns, the outside pressure is applied throughout the arc of the turn, and then transferred to the new outside ski for the change in direction. This fundamental concept is key to turning. You can mentally picture this by having the old outside leg flex and after finishing the turn to reduce pressure, while at the same time the new outside leg extends and lengthens. This extending of the leg increases the pressure on to the new outside ski thus, completing the transfer pressure cycle. In simple kid's terms, it's like *riding the bicycle*—long leg/short leg.

It is important to know that by extending the outside leg, the COM moves *across* the BOS towards the *inside* tip of the skis and *inside* the turn. This allows the long leg to create an edge angle and pressure and the short leg to flatten the ski to allow gravity to pull the downhill ski into the turn. Another approach you can use to teach pressure control is to flex both legs at different rates through the transition from one turn to the next. The old outside leg flexes at a faster rate than the new outside leg. With this method, the COM lowers or remains level with the ground as weight is transferred and the COM and BOS realign. This can occur in bumps and other variable terrain, and in dynamic short-radius-turn maneuvers.

Pressure control has a unique relationship with *balance*. The skier must maintain equilibrium to stay in dynamic balance while adding pressure to bend the skis to allow the change in direction. By adjusting the student's stance to remain in balance during turns, you need to continually make adjustments to increase, decrease, or maintain pressure on the skis. How can you check the senior's pressure control? Quite simple: I call it the "*Gloved-Hand Under the Ski Test*".

Place your gloved hand under the tip region of the ski and have the student apply pressure (Closing the ankles) and check if the child can add varying amounts of pressure onto your gloved hand. You will find that many seniors cannot apply enough strength to the front cuff of the booth to get the ski tips to engage in the snow to begin the turn initiation. Unlike the adult that is doing dynamic turns, the senior student is doing less angles (More upright stance) for the athletic stance to allow the stacking of the bones for more efficient turns.

Rotational Control[25]

*R*efers to turning the skis about the vertical axis of the body. This skill highlights the ability of a skier to control the change in direction of the skis. Be aware of *leg rotation* and *counter rotation. Leg rotation* is defined as a movement of the lower body to affect the direction the skis point. This includes elements of rotation from the femur in the hip socket and lower-leg or below the knee (Ankle) rotation. The upper body should be the anchor (Stable point) for the rotation to be effective. For example, visualize a grandfather clock, the pendulum will not swing properly if the upper portion of the clock is unstable. Thus, keep the upper body stable so that the lower body can articulate the movements to affect the skis to change direction. Because instability and balance are issues for the elderly, teach them to use their poles more by reaching downhill to do turn around the poles: this forms a tripod (Two skis and the ski pole) which gives more stability of the upper body.

Counter rotation

Describes the upper body turns in one direction and the lower body (Hip and legs) turns in the opposite direction. Some call this *Anticipation*, which describes a position or anticipatory movements in preparation for turning. In this case, the upper body actively turns to face downhill rather than across the hill in the direction the skis are pointing. This process is necessary to stretch and engage muscles for the turn. Counter rotation not only provides more edge angles, but assists with the turning because the lower body is 'twisted' from the upper body and the lower body want to unwind to a neutral position. The upper-body rotation alone is typically an inefficient movement. The proper sequence is as follows: the upper body turns first, followed by the legs turning in the same direction as the lower body unwinds. The separation of the upper body and lower body will assist in the turns. Inexperienced skiers tend to use the whole upper body twisting technique to get the lower body to turn via the inertia of the upper body. Some seniors do this because they do not have the proper body developments or use inappropriate movements (Because of the lack of knowledge) to initiate the turn, (e.g., The elders may use the person's upper body to "swing" into the turn). As a coach, you should be aware that depending on the age and physical condition of the person, they have not developed the upper- and lower-body separation, and are more "one-body" in their rotational movements because of a spinal fusion. Why? Because their neuro-musculature development dictates that type of movement, because of his/her arthritis.

So, for the time being, focus on the lower body by getting the skis to point in the direction of the turns (Rotational skills) until the person has more cognitive and physical developments.

When skiing parallel, both corresponding edges are released simultaneously as both skis are tipped into the turn. The BOS needs to stay under the COS; this is done by pulling the skis slightly back and manage the rebound energy through retraction. When the COS is aligned properly over the BOS, you are in much better dynamic balance. A majority of the skiers push the skis slightly forward at the end of a turn; you have just lost balance and power by not being able to flex the ankles enough to pressure the edges. Another issue that contributes to ineffective turn initiation is skiers lack the patience to let the ski seek the fall line; instead, most skiers push the skis (Heels) laterally to get the skis out of the fall line as quickly as possible, thus, interrupting the ability to shape the turn. Great skiers possess the ability to shape turns in the control phase and are so refined that they can adjust the arc of the turn while they are in it by employing **DIRT** (**D**uration, **I**ntensity, **R**ate, and **T**iming) of the skills applied during the turn. More information on rotational control can be found in chapter 9.

Balance[25]

What is Balance? Simply put, it is the body's attempt to maintain equilibrium in basically, an upright position by conscious and nonconscious (Automatic) reflexes. There are four key body parts that are involved in balance: three sensory organs (Eyes, inner ear, and proprioceptors), and the brain, where incoming information from the three sensors is forwarded to the processing and control center, which is the brain. Proprioception is the body's sense of self-movement and body position. These highly specialized sensory organs send messages to the brain about the limb's velocity and movements, the amount of load on a limb, and the limb limits. These complex series of neuromuscular networks account for knowing where our body parts are in the environment, and to help maintain a desired position. Observe figure 5 (Stick drawing[24] of a perfect athletic stance) and try to mimic that posture in front of the mirror daily. Remember, for the elderly, the COM is higher because the student stands taller to allow the bones to stack. Practice, practice, practice the right fundamental movements. All athletes practice fundamental movements intensely with the guidance of a skilled coach. Like golf, my coach once told me that, *"Practice is useless if you don't practice the proper skills and mechanics of the golf swing. If you don't, when you go to the practice range, all that you will do is just reinforce bad habits"*.

Other Considerations on Balance

A common debate is whether being in a state of dynamic balance creates the ability to move more effectively by using the other three skills, or vice versa. The answer for this dual role of balance is "yes." In addition, you need to recognize the interdependent relationship between the skills and balance, the results of effective and efficient movements. Since the majority of your students are out of balance (Usually in the 'back seat' of the middle of the skis), focus your attention on this movement skill.

When I communicate to a child, I ask the child, "When your parents drive the car are they in the front seat or back seat?" Invariably the answer is, "In the front seat." Then, I tell them, "Well, you're driving those skis, you'd better be in the front seat of your skis!" "If you are not in the front seat, you will lose control and the skis will run away. I'll inform the elderly the same story—maybe it'll give him/her a clearer mental picture on what it means to be up front"

Because, PSIA and AASI have made gradual modifications over the years by NOT considering *balance* as a skill, but rather an outcome of developing the blended elements (Skills) of the edge control, pressure control, and rotary control, do examine how we use these elements *in The Five Fundamentals of Skiing* throughout the text. More discussion on balancing skills can be found in chapter 9.

Photo 6. Older gentleman with great athletic stance and is doing beautiful C-shaped turns in a parallel platform.

Photo 7. 65 year-old woman with great athletic stance.

How can we translate the physiological definition of balance into a practical and realistic definition? Since the majority of an instructor's focus in working on balance during various activities, let's break the movements down into segments. In this discussion I will utilize the *Five Fundamentals of Skiing*[25] (Which is discussed extensively in this section in this chapter) to illustrate the movements necessary for turning. In a static exercise, balance begins with the upper torso, head, arms and hands (Called the center of mass, *COM*) are centered directly over the foot arch (Called the base of support, *BOS*) so that there is equal pressure on the entire foot, from the toes to the heels. In an **athletic stance**[12] the body is in a readiness position. Here, the COM moves slightly forward by flexing (Closing) the ankles so that the knees move forward along with the COM and the pressure on the foot moves to the center of the arch of the feet, and sometimes towards to the ball of the foot, depending on how aggressive one is skiing and other conditions. Since we spend the majority of our time teaching turning maneuvers of different shapes, size, and speed, let us focus on *balance* as we go through the different phases of the turn. ***Four Phases of the Turn***

There are *four phases of the Turn*: (1) Phase 0 or *Transition Phase,* which is not usually mentioned in the PSIA manual, (2) Phase 1 or *Turn Initiation*, (3) Phase 2 or *Shaping of the Turn*, and (4) Phase 3 or *Finishing of the Turn.*

Photo 8. This older person had a nasty crash from the loss of speed control because the movement analysis of the left ski's is convex-shaped instead of concave-shaped.

Transition Phase

While this is an often times neglected discussion, this is an important phase of the turn. Many skiers are out of balance as they finish a turn and enter this regrouping Transition phase. If one is out of alignment and balance, there are couple of things that one can accomplish to re-center the COM over the BOS during this phase. One is flexing (Closing) the ankles to get the COM over the BOS, and second to pull both feet (BOS) back under the COM. Most skiers tend to rush going from one turn to the next without giving themselves enough time to regroup. One of the drills that I have the students do is the *2-4-2* Edge Concept. Give sufficient amount of time when the student has four edges on the snow to allow time to get back into balance, so that one can begin the turn initiation more effectively with edges engaged from both skis.

A yoga teacher once taught me how to get more flexibility and pliability in my ankles and more ankle strength by sitting down on a stool or chair, stretch the ankle ligaments and muscles by pointing the toes forward, then backward as far as you can, isometrically. Repeat that exercise 15 minutes daily. The second exercise is doing counter rotation and clockwise rotation for 15 minutes in each direction. I highly recommend both of these ankle exercises to seniors because they simply don't get enough exercise and they simply can't get their COM forward enough to be balanced over the BOS. Seniors seem to complain a lot about been stiff, perhaps because of arthritis.

Turn Initiation

The beginner skier in the wedge platform can begin to initiate the turn by moving the COM diagonally towards the inside (Downhill) skis tip. This causes the outside (Uphill) leg to lengthen and the inside (Downhill) leg to actively retract—like pedaling the bicycle (e.g., Push down on one pedal as the other pedal moves up) or doing heavy foot/light foot drill. The skis will react by the outside ski having more edge angle and pressure to initiate a change in direction of the ski. The inside leg is actively shortened and is thereby closer to the center of the body with little or no edge angle (Almost flattened on the snow). This causes the ski to release the contralateral edge to disengage from the snow and allow gravity to pull the inside tip downhill as the uphill or outside ski follows. The movements for the parallel skier follow the same sequence of events except that both corresponding edges engage the

56

snow at relatively the same time and causes both skis to change direction in unison. With both the wedge and parallel skier the rotary skill is also used to blend with the edging and pressure skill to start the turn. It is key to remember that weight transfer shifts from a neutral position to the outside ski and one should be balanced throughout the turn on that one ski.

Don't forget the *tripod* effect during the turn-inition phase of the turn.

Shaping of the Turn

This is the fastest phase of the turn because of the amount of time that is spent in the fall line. The greatest speed and force occur at the apex of the arc. The speed is determined by the turn shape (See figure 11) and by the size of the wedge (See figure 13). The wedge stance is slower than the parallel platform. The shape, size and speed of the turn is determined by *DIRT*.

Figure 5. The different shaped turns (S, C, and J) will affect speed control.

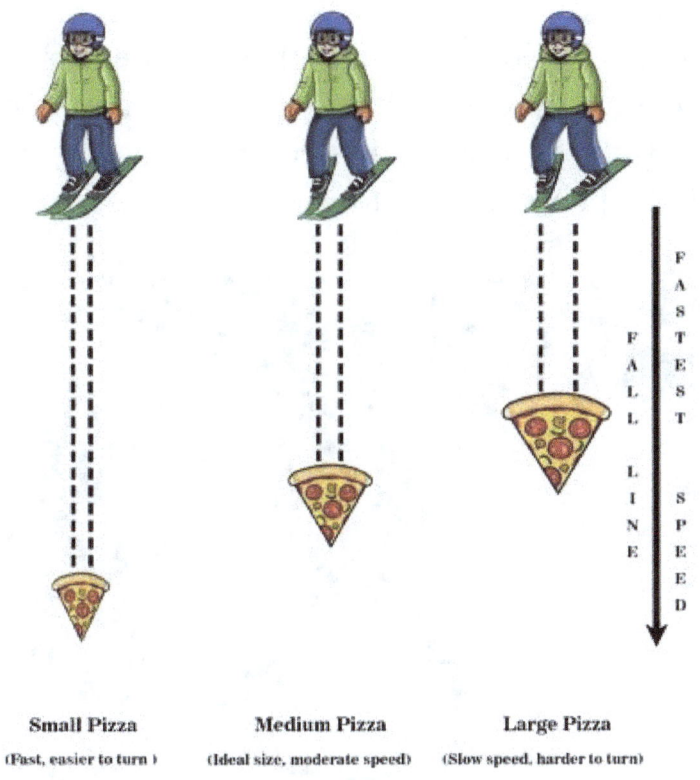

Small Pizza   Medium Pizza   Large Pizza

(Fast, easier to turn)   (Ideal size, moderate speed)   (Slow speed, harder to turn)

Figure 6. The different sizes of Pizzas will affect the speed.

Figure 7. The speed is slower when using a wedge platform compared to a parallel platform.

Finishing the Turn

The major objective of the finishing phase of the turn is to control one's speed. Many students do not finish their turns and they tend to pick up too much speed and get out of balance and control. Coaches should emphasize the importance of this phase of the turn.

Photo 9. This 59 year-old autistic woman lost her balance by not finishing her turns, which caused her to lose speed control and crashed into the safety net. This was fortunate because behind the net was a brick house. Next time ski tools (Poles, plastic hoops, ski harness should be used so she can practice safely her completed turns to maintain constant speed.

Photo 10. Many seniors do not like speed. Keep them on a flat terrain and begin teaching them the fundamentals of turning. Their number one challenge and concern is falling because of the difficulty of getting up.

Photo 11. Gradually expose them to steeper terrain, making controlled C-turns; be sure that they finish the turns to control their speed.

Five Fundamentals of Skiing Model[25]

This section will provide you with a short overview of this important model. Additional readings are provided in the references.

Direct Pressure to the outside ski and pressure control from ski-to-ski

Transferring your weight to the outside or inside ski and being balanced is not an easy feat. After finishing a turn, it is a fundamental goal to get balanced over the downhill or outside ski or balanced over the uphill or inside ski. When making a right turn, it is a left-footed turn, and when making a left turn, it is a right-footed turn. Pressure increase/decrease can be achieved couple of ways; one of which is by lengthening the leg, or by shortening the leg. The ankles (Opening and closing) and the knees both play a major role in extension and flexing motion. Retraction of the legs is another way for adjusting the pressure on the skis. Do not neglect the proper position of the hips relative to the BOS when focusing on balance. Drills that can be utilized for this fundamental skill is discussed further in chapter 9.

Control Edge Angles with Inclination and Angulation

Tipping the skis onto their edges, involves inclining the body toward the inside of the turn in the direction you are turning; it also involves angulating the upper body back toward the skis (Towards the outside of the turn). When making a right turn, move the uphill hip and shoulder up; keep the downhill hip and shoulder down. The opposite movements are done with a left turn. The COS needs to move in the direction of the turn. As discussed in the Skill Concept Model, edging can be achieved through inclination, angulation, or both. The foot or ankle articulation also plays a role in edging. Drills for this fundamental skill is discussed further in chapter 9.

Keeping the COM over the BOS

Controlling the COM to stay over the BOS is always a challenge during any type of skiing. Staying in balance to utilize the entire length of the skis, the front of the skis and the back of the skis when need, is a tough fundamental to master. The results of this control, are better stability and balance; and better control on how the skis turn. Staying in balance in the center of the skis is your primary goal.

Controlling the Skis' Rotation

This can be achieved by (Turning, pivoting, steering) with leg rotation that is separate from the upper body. The upper body (Including the core) should be quiet and stable, while the lower body rotates independently by twisting the femur (Upper leg) in the hip socket to the right or to the left.

Regulate the Magnitude of Pressure Created through Ski/Snow Interactions

You can create resistance by pushing down on the snow. The force a ski puts into the snow acts at a right angle to its surface. The reaction force also acts at a right angle to the base of the ski. There are two things that you can do with a ski which will affect the reaction force and its components. The first is to tilt a ski onto its edge, and the second is to change the direction that a ski is pointing in along its length. As a ski's resistance comes from the ski's reaction from the snow, two forces can push the ski into the snow, gravity, and a momentum-induced force from changing your velocity. Gravity always acts straight downwards with a set force. The momentum induced force will only act if you are changing velocity; this creates a Gforce as we turn. This is a difficult topic to understand, but whenever you go out skiing, focus on these forces that create pressure. Try to determine how the pressure skills are interwoven into the *Five Fundamentals of Skiing Model.*[25]

When contemplating an activity, ask these questions of yourself:
• **What** movement pattern will we be practicing?
• **Why** are we going to perform this activity?
• **How** will it enhance my lesson and affect our skiing today?
• **Where** are we going to do the drills?

When you factor these four questions into you lesson plans, you have involved a **Better Mechanics of Learning**.

In addition, remember the following three key pillars[21]: *1)*
People Skills Fundamentals

• Develop relationships built on trust.
•• Engage in meaningful two-way communications.
• Identify, understand, and manage your emotions and actions.
• Recognize and influence the behaviors, motivations, and emotions of others.

2) Teaching Fundamentals

• Collaborate on long-term goals and short-term objectives.
• Manage information, activities, terrain selection, and pacing.
• Promote play, experimentation, and exploration.
• Facilitate the learner's ability to reflect upon experiences and sensations.
• Adapt to the changing needs of the learner.
• Manage emotional and physical risks.

3) The Five Alpine Fundamentals

• Control the relationship of the Center of Mass to the Base of Support todirect pressure along the length of the skis.
• Control pressure from ski to ski and direct pressure towards the outside ski.
• Control edge angles through a combination of inclination and angulation.

- Control the skis' rotation (Turning, pivoting, steering) with leg rotation, separate from the upper body.
- Regulate the magnitude of pressure created through ski/snow interaction.

Chapter 8

Teaching The ABC's of Safety

As we stated in chapter 6, to bond with the senior student, you need to promise them that *safety* is highest on your coaching agenda. There are over three-hundred million snow sport enthusiasts throughout the world, and accidents do happen. It is estimated that over 600,000 injuries are reported each year nationally, as a result of skiing and snowboarding. Make sure that you fully understand your ski resort's safety policy. Indicate how you intend to implement this into your lesson plans. Later, at the closing, explain to the friends and elderly how and where you taught *safety*.

Every ski resort has their version of the Responsibility Code[4-7, 12, 18, 25]

A. Above: Always be visible to skiers *above* you.

B. Breaks: Be sure to have *ski brakes* working and retention strap on your skis poles to prevent runaway equipment.

C. Control: Be sure you ski in *control* at all times.

D. Downhill: The *downhill* skier has the right-of-way; do not collide into them, If you are going to overtake them, say out loud, "S*kier on your left or right.*"

E. Enter: *Enter* trails safely—whenever starting downhill or merging on a new trail, always *look uphill* and yield.

F. Follow: *Follow* all *posted signs*, stay off of *closed trails.*

G. Get: *Get* on and off the chairlifts safely. Know how to load, ride and unload the *chair and conveyer belt* properly and safely.

If you want to cut to the chase and simplify your Safety presentation, try using my modified version of what Deer Valley Ski Resort uses[28] I modified it to DUCKS'S:

D = *Downhill* skier has the right-of-way.

U = *Always* look *up the hill* before pulling out.

C = *Always* ski in c*ontrol.*

K = *Know* and follow all the rules and posted signs.

S = *Stop* where you can be visible from above.

S = *Safely load,* ride, and unload the children onto the people mover conveyer belt and chairlift.

Other Safety Guidelines

There are *other safety issues* that need special attention with COVID-19. With the viral air-born pandemic, the ski industry is going through a major revolution for safety.[14] In conjunction with the National Ski Areas Association (NSAA) and PSIA/AASI encourages everyone to follow the national guidelines, "Ski Well, Be Well" (nsaa.org@skiwellbewell). Review periodic guidelines for safety updates that are aligned with the Centers for Disease Control & Prevention (Atlanta, Georgia) (tiny.cc@COVID19CDCGuidelines.com). This is your responsibility! All ski resorts all over the world are struggling to maintain the pandemic safety and have posted many rules for protection; this has been a year of experimentation for survival.[2] There are other ways that you can help protect yourself from this requirement improve the quality of your sleep, avoid tobacco, drink less alcohol, minimize stress, weight gain, increase your physical activity, and improve the frequency of sanitizing your ski gloves when teaching. There is absolutely no doubt that wearing a mask and social distancing are worthy protection.

I have discovered that there are at least three compromises when you are coaching and wearing a mask. (1) You will have difficulty communicating; your students; they cannot hear you are saying and you cannot hear them. The mask will act like a car muffler to reduce the engine noise. So, at the very beginning of the lesson, you need to carefully explain that you will try to speak *louder* and more *clearly*; if they cannot hear you, inform them that they should say, "Please repeat that, coach." You may want to step back and temporarily pull your mask away from your lip and let the volume of air and sound out to more readily reach your student(s). The student can do the same thing so that you can also hear them. I can't imagine the struggles that we will go through when all the snow guns are making snow! (2) It will be extremely difficult to show emotions besides jumping down, clapping your hands, doing other body movements to show signs of approval, excitement and acceptance. Since every child seeks a beautiful smile of approval, you may want to temporarily lower the mask to show your smile. Today there are creative manufacturers that are making face masks that are made of clear plastic so people can see your facial expressions. (3) When you are skiing hard and seem to be out of breath, try lowering the mask and take two to three minutes of deep breathing to reoxygenate your lungs.

Other safety issue include

1. Do not coach your students under the chairlifts because of the possibilities of falling equipment.

2. Coach them to not bomb the hill at Mach-2 speeds for fear of not being able to stop when a person unexpectantly changes direction in front of them. About 54% of the deaths occurred on blue (Intermediate), groomed runs; 31% were on Expert trails. Remember 69% of the accidents were on beginner and intermediate trails. Most of the accidents were males between the ages of 18 and 40. I have personally observed seniors in their early 50s charge down the hill at high speeds and get hurt. It always pays to inform them to be cautious.

3. Emphasize slowing down into the lift line, instead of zooming ahead, so you do not have to spend extra time and energy standing in line or are too lazy to shuffle ahead.

4. Reduce the odds of getting into an accident by avoiding the section of the hill that is crowded or congested. Skiing and snowboarding are not contact sports; however, in reality, people do collide into one another. Minimize distractions; sometimes listening to music or having earbuds to take a mobile phone call can increase your risk for collisions.

5. People have a tendency to play on the ride up on the chair. Avoid any unnecessary movements that can cause a student to slide off the chair; this is especially true when all the snow guns are making snow and the chair has snow on it and it freezes, making it extra slippery.

6. It is becoming increasingly popular to carry a backpack, containing essentials such as water bottles, snacks, extra pair of goggles, cell phones, radios. When riding the chairlifts, take the backpack off and place it in your lap. There have been reported cases of backpacks getting tangled on the back of the chairlift resulting in accidents.

7. Avoid taking them into the terrain park if you have not been trained to play in the park safely. About 27% of the accidents occur in the terrain park; mostly due to freestyle skiing.

Photo 12. A 50-year-old gentleman doing less-dangerous tricks in the terrain park.

Photo 13. This 54-year-old advanced skier is doing some dangerous tricks in the terrain park.

8. Ensure your students are cognitively, affectively, and physically ready to challenge themselves down a steeper terrain with the proper skills to go down in control and safely, especially on the 'last run' when they are exhausted from a long ski lesson.

9. Never push your students beyond their mental and physical limits; this is especially true if they are tired or exhausted, at the end of the lesson. Don't be afraid for a short 'time out' even though the time of the lesson is not over.

10. Always check periodically that *Maslow's Hierarchy of Needs*,[17, 27] especially the physiological and safety needs are not being met; the child can be easily distracted and not obey what is being told when they have higher physiological or mental needs.

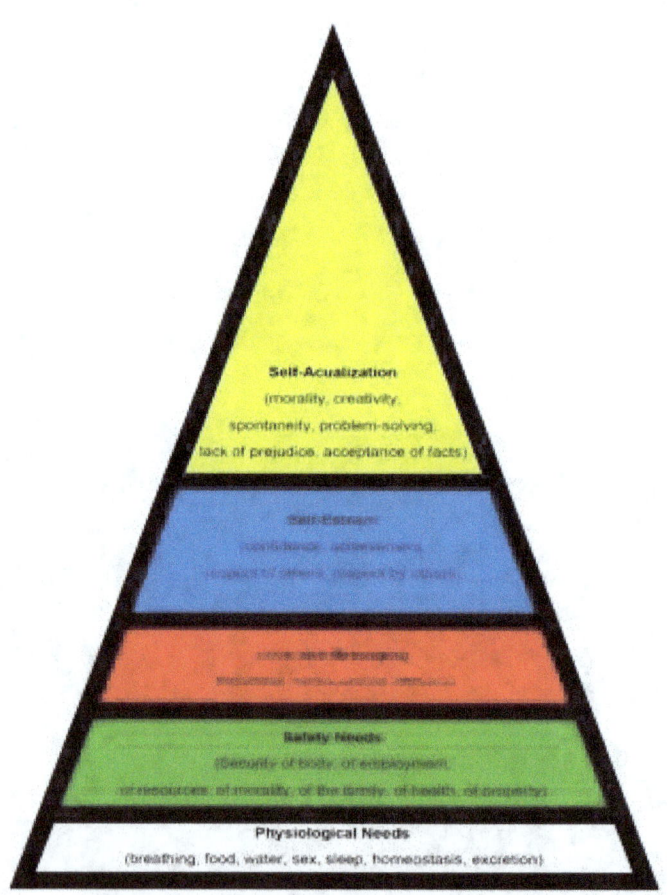

Figure 8. Maslow's Hierarchy of Needs

11. Pay special attention to those individuals that need more care, such as those with certain physical, mental, neurological disorders or diseases and those that are on special medications. Do ask, "Has your grandpa/grandma been

properly fed? Has she/he received their daily medications before going out on the slopes? Also, being a diabetic myself, I always keep sufficient rapidly-sugar cubes in my pocket in the event that my sugar plummets. Some diabetic children keep sugar tabs or candy in their pockets in the event hypoglycemia (Low blood sugar) occurs. Ideally, before taking any sugar product, testing the sugar level with a glucometer is recommended. The dropping blood sugar can result in the loss of cognition very rapidly (Usually within a few minutes). Do try to recognize the symptoms of low sugar in the blood (See chapter 8, under "Diabetes").

12. I also recommend carrying a small pack of tissue in your pocket in the event a senior citizen tot needs any assistance with a runny nose. Wintertime is flu season so, also keep a small bottle of hand sanitizer handy, especially in this era of new airborne viruses. Frequent disinfecting the hands *and* gloves will be the new norm for the future. Little things like this can avoid distractions and can lead to a better outcome of a critical and challenging situation.

13. Teach the seniors how to carry their skis properly when walking to and from the ski lodge. As this is a high-traffic area, be especially careful when changing direction so that you do not hit someone else.

14. Never borrow someone else's skis; the DIN setting may not be correct for your height, weight, age, and level skier you are.

15. Another safety issue can be conquering *fear* itself.[12] Fear can be a terrifying thing, preventing a person from trying something new, or sitting back (The COM is behind the BOS), or letting emotions get out of hand and the child refuses any more instructions or wants to go back to their parents. Fear can, sometimes, be good, promoting caution in dangerous circumstances, like a steeper slope or going into the terrain park. There are some kids that have no fear and they can be a real hazard on the hill. As we get older, we file more fear factors and experiences into our brain. Some of the files are overfilled! You can keep the student on a lower terrain doing different drills to hone in on their skills. Eventually, that same terrain will become boring. Now, the challenge sets in on introducing the new steeper terrain. On a less-steeper terrain, you may want to try the fan turns. Tell the student that going straight down the fall-line (With the speed increasing may be too much), they can bail out and make a J- turn. To put it another way, as the straight runs get

longer, the speed enhances, but they can always bail out and do a J-Turn. When the student understands there is a safety net (By turning uphill), they can bail out of the calamity. Do repeat the J-turn drill several more times to help concur the fears. Another exercise that you can do is do it on a less-steep terrain. Be sure to check their *turn shapes* and their balance on the skis to determine why the person is picking up so much speed (See figures 4-6)[5, 18, 25] Some of the other fears besides speed, are heights and jumps. Do you know how the different-shaped turns affect speed? How does S-shaped turns, a C-shaped turns, or J-shaped turns affect speed? More on speed control is found in chapter 8.

Figure 9. Snow Sport Motto: Safety, Fun, Learning

16. Don't be surprised when you have a client or two who are seniors that want to do heliskiing. They are advanced-performance level skiers that are in terrific condition. The maintain their body weight by eating healthy and they exercise daily and seek adventurous skiing.

Photo 14. This 62-year-old gent is doing heliskiing for an adventurous ride down the mountain.

Going against gravity to slow down is key to controlling your speed, so understanding turn shapes[5, 18] is a mandate. The S-Shaped[5, 18] turns should be reserved for more accomplished skiers who can turn in control their turns at faster speeds. The C-shaped turns should be taught to the beginner and intermediate skiers to help them move up the hill against gravity to slow down. But they must finish the turn and go up the slope against gravity. Without slowing down, the body soon gets out of alignment with the skis, and compromises balance and the other skills. Turning then becomes a challenge. One of the games which I like to do with the students is to see who can go down the slope the *slowest* by making the most turns and by completing the turns to slow down. I personally, compete with them to add to the extra fun. As discussed previously, the J-shaped turns are a good way to build confidence against fear. In addition, the fan turn drill is excellent for this. As you well know the fall-line is the fastest line for speed. The J-turn[5, 18] is an excellent way for the student to come to a complete stop. The super-large wedge should be reserved for emergency stops only (i.e., In the lift line or in a crowded area when a hockey stop is not advised). Besides, a super-large wedge promotes the COM be in the back of the BOS position causing imbalance. Figure 7 illustrates how staying in the fall line picks up speed, but one can bail out when the speed is excessive, by making J-Turns[5,18] to come to a complete stop. This can be a good drill to help conquer fears of speed down the fall line. One of the things that I tell my students is, *"Speed causes injuries. That is why they have safe speed limits in the city and on the highways. When your grandparents exceed the speed limits, they can get a speeding ticket and you can get one too from the snow patrol. So, always ski safely by going slow."*

There are several ways of implementing **speed control**:

1. The student should only use terrain steepness that matches his/her skill level.
2. Apply the J-turns to go the slowest and come to a stop after the turn.
3. Apply the C-turns to go at moderate speeds.
4. Apply the S-turns to go at faster speeds.
5. The student must finish the turns for the different shaped turns to work.
6. Use the wedge turns rather than the parallel platform to go slower.
7. Use the entire hill by traversing the entire hill and adjusting the speed by going uphill or going downhill.
8. Do spend the time to inform the adaptive adults and seniors to not bomb the hill at Mache 2 speeds because of dire consequences.
9. Experiment with Fan turns to help conquer fear, by making a series of longer J-turns and finishing the turns to come to a complete stop (The bailout). The elderly can go down the fall line and pick up speed until fear starts to set in, and they can then bailout. Be mindful that the elderly considers a successful day is **NOT FALLING!**

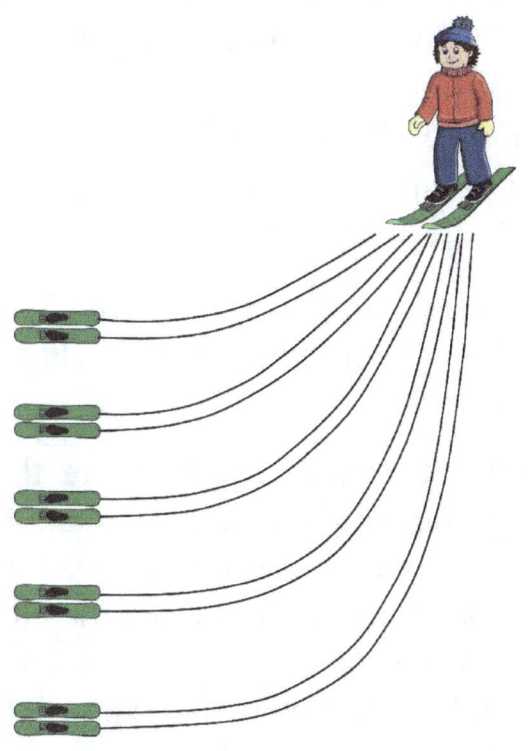

Figure 10. Fan turns: making different size J-turns to help conquer fear of speed.

In case of an *accident*, the following *rules* should be observed:

• Do not touch or move the injured person.

• Do not remove any of their equipment.

• Ask someone to tell the lift operator to call the ski patrol

• Stay with the student.

• Put your skis in an 'X' high above the injured person to prevent a collision from oncoming traffic above.

• Have the hill supervisor (Or other management staff member) assign another instructor to take over the class.

• Accompany the injured student to the ski patrol hut to complete the necessary paper work

Try to immediately locate the senior's relatives or family to inform them of the accident; call the front desk at the resort (Follow the resort's policy). Do not overlook the senior's *preparation* for the snow. Many seniors do not have the latest technology on clothing nor equipment. As their coach you need to inform your client of the essentials of dressing for the typical cold weather,

74

blizzard conditions, subzero weather, the elements of the wind, blowing snow from the snow guns, rain, and so on. Here is *a brief checklist* when preparing for the outdoors:

1. The concept of layering the clothing: base layer, mid-layer, outer layer that is windproof, waterproof and can breathe (See discussion on "clothing" in this chapter).

2. Pay attention to the material composition selected: wool, silk, and synthetic materials help with the wicking process and to help retain body heat. Do not use cotton materials.

3. Socks should preferably be changed just before the lesson. The feet are continuously perspiring, some kids' feet more than others. If you put the ski socks on before they leave the house, many times they will be damp with perspiration, which will lead to cold feet when the child gets on the snow on a bitter cold day. Warm weather during the spring lessons, may require removing the outer layer; be prepared with the proper mid-layer to keep them warm, but not hot. I say you should consider the outer layer first because many times it is made up of down feathers, which can be great for bitter cold weather, but not for warm spring weather skiing. An alternative, if they are wearing a thinner outer shell, you can remove one of the mid layers. Make sure that the pants and gloves are breathable to minimize the accumulation of perspiration, are water-proof and wind-proof because they are most likely to get wet. No jeans!

4. Be sure they their neck area are protected from the elements; avoid scarves and wraps for safety reasons (Discussed else ware in this book). A turtle-neck sweater can do the job. Because of the COVID-19 pandemic, you may want to consider recommending to the parent and child to wear a full-cover balaclava, which will protect the entire face and neck area. The goggles will protect the eyes and the rest of the face.

5. Neoprene face masks are always helpful for subzero weather. They are usually thicker than the balaclava fabric, and will help protect most of the face, head, and ears from the cold, and even from frostbit.

6. Inform them on the many uses of a properly fitted helmet. It doesn't take much to obtain a concussion; snow sport is an active sport. A person will lose

50-60 percent of their body heat via the head. It is always wise to purchase helmets with adjustable vents to allow heat to escape when the weather gets warmer. The more expensive helmets have a more sophisticated acoustical design, whereby the person can hear better.

7. Check their goggles; are they the correct size and shape to fit the contour of their faces. Goggles not only keep a large portion of their face warmer, but also keeps the flying snow and other particles from getting into their eyes. Know the signs of frostbite (See chapter 8, under "Frostbite"). Because this is a very common and serious problem. I would like to spend more time on this important subject because children are particularly susceptible because of several reasons:
   - Seniors lose heat from their thin skin and particularly from their head.
   - Seniors with ailments can get so excited and engrossed in playing in the snow that they lose track of what is happening to their bodies, or simply ignore how cold or uncomfortable they continue to have uninterrupted fun.
   - An elderly person may not have the cognitive skills that are impaired to alert them to the symptoms of *frostbite* and how to prevent them (e.g., Taking a break and seeking warm shelter).
   - Seniors also have thinner skin and have less blood flow on the surface tissues that make them colder than adults.

Because of these reasons, your senior clients must especially be attentive to:
1. Monitoring the weather forecast, outdoor temperature, wind velocity, and wind-chill factor.
2. Asking frequent questions from the knowledgeable coach.
3. Allowing and planning periodic warm-up time in a warm shelter and offer warm fluids and food.

Frostnip and *Frostbites* can be a common occurrence in this winter sport.

Frostbite

Refers to freezing of the body skin and underlying tissues caused by extreme cold. This can result in the loss of feeling and color in the tissues.

There are three degrees of frostbite:
- *Frostnip*: white patches of skin that are numb
- *Superficial frostbite*: skin that is white and hard; deeper skin, blood vessels, and nerve injury with a burning and stinging sensation; clear waterfilled blisters that may develop when the skin is re-warmed.

• **Deep frostbite**: grayish-yellow or blue skin and feels hard or waxy; larger blood vessels and nerves, muscles, tendons, and bone injury occur with the loss of sensation; gangrene and infection may develop.

What should you do? First of all, *prevention* is key. Recognize the symptoms and take quick action. Check the exposed areas of the skin; is there redness, or any other color or lack of color? Skin with frostnip starts out being red and later turns pale, cold and hard with no feeling. Does the client feel "pins and needles"? This sensation is followed by numbness, and this may lead to an early throbbing or aching feeling. Later on, the affected parts feel like a "block of wood". Do they show signs of being cold? It's time to bring them in immediately! The most common areas of the body that are affected include the fingers and toes (Which account for 90 percent of the cases), nose, lips, cheeks and ears follow. Some medical conditions such as diabetes, peripheral vascular disease, Renaud's Syndrome, hypothyroidism (low thyroid function), some forms of heart problems can result in increased susceptibility to frostbites. Be especially attentive when the snow guns are blowing 'sticky' snow and it adheres to the body; the high winds and cold can potentially add to increased risk of frostnip or frostbite.

To summarize the *symptoms* of frostbite:
• Redness of the skin
• Loss of skin color
• Blue skin color
• Graying or blackening of the affected areas
• Feeling 'pins and needles'
• Local numbness
• Local blisters
• Local swelling• Shivering
• Slurred speech
• Memory loss

Be aware that a person with frostbite on the extremities may also be subjected to hypothermia (Lowered body core temperature). Check for hypothermia and treat these symptoms first. In this instance, it would be best that you call the ski patrol or admit the child to the emergency room. Also, if your child has had frostnip or frostbite previously, he/she will be five-times more sensitive to the cold and more prone to have a repeated event.

What should you do for *treatment*? Work swiftly:

- Get the person out of the wind and cold.
- Move the client to a warm shelter.
- Remove any wet or damp clothing, mittens, and socks when you get indoors.
- Remove any constricting jewelry.
- Remove any tight clothing or clothing that may restrict blood flow.
- Apply slow warming with blankets and warm clothing.
- Do *not* rub or massage the frostbitten areas.
- Do not let the child walk on the frostbitten feet.
- Do *not* apply any direct heat to the area.
- Do *not* sit by a warm fire.
- Do *not* warm the person with an electric blanket.
- Do *not* break the blisters.
- Do provide ample warm fluids.
- Preventive antibiotic medications may be necessary per the advice of the doctor.
- Pain medications may be necessary.
- Treatment for general hypothermia may be necessary.
- Common sense should dictate when and where the extreme cold weather forecast is in the making. As their coach you need to take the leadership in preventing these types of mishaps.

Chapter 9

How to Create Successful Lesson Plans for Senior Citizens

As a reminder, there are several things that stand out in coaching senior citizens skiing.

A major goal for seniors is having fun and socializing and simplifying the low-impact but continuous movement lesson plans.

Photo 15. Do not underestimate the elderly group taking enough breaks and socializing.

Photo 16. As part of this woman's ritual is an evening of relaxation with a nice glass of red wine next to a warm fire place.

79

Photo 17. This gentleman's challenge is not getting to the hot tub, but getting to his resort hotel room in sufficient time to protect his private parts!

Photo 18. After a hard-day skiing, try renting a tour guide and a bunch of snowmobiles to have fun with your buddies as the sun sets to view the gorgeous sunset.

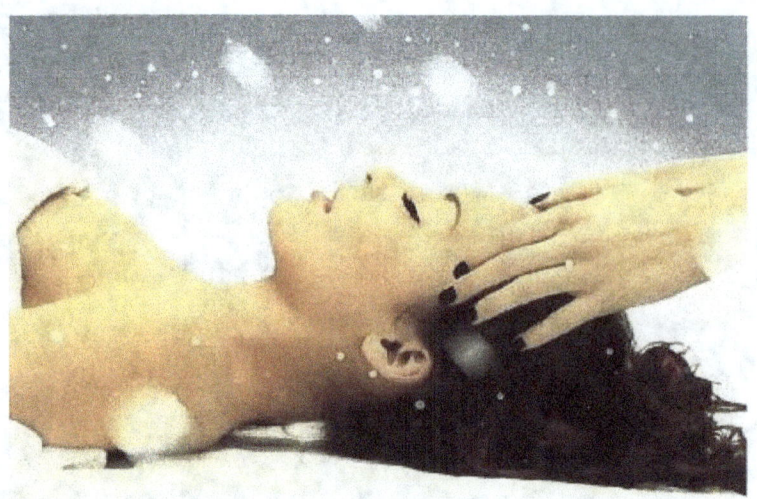

Photo 19. Don't worry ladies, you can immerse yourself into a Spa and get a relaxing facial massage.

Safety is another major concern for most senior clients. Be sure to discuss and inform them all of the ways to ski safely (See chapter 8) and especially speed control. Be sure to also discuss how shape of the turns can influence speed:

. S-Turns: These turns are for faster speed while making turns down the hill. I focus on the turns being the same size (About a fifteen to twenty feet corridor width.

.C-Turns: This is the "bread and butter turn" for medium-controlled speed down the slope. I focus on the child finishing the turn to help keep the speed constant.

. J-Turns: As mentioned before, this is a great turn shape for making a turn and coming to a stop. Blend this turn into the progressive fan turns to help alleviate fear of speeds.

Figure 11. If you get tired and exhausted, take a break so you don't crash and interrupt your evening events.

Photo 20. *Be mindful that the last thing on the senior's wish list is getting injured.*

Some senior clients change their minds when they get to the ski resorts after seeing another senior getting hurt, despite a senior-specialist coach is trying to convenience the person that safely will be a big part of the lesson.

Challenge: This 80-year old advanced-beginner woman has difficulty controlling her speed down the hill.

Solution: There are several things you can teach to migitate this issue: (1) move the person to a lower grade slope, (2) have her practice J-turns, (3) focus on finishing the turns, (4) be sure she is in good athletic stance throughout the turn; without that she will be out of balance and will have difficulty executing the three skills to get the skis to finish the turns while in balance.

Challenge: A 50-year-old woman is having difficulty coming to a stop because she is on her heels; thus, out of balance.

Solution: Work on a static drill on first showing her what a proper athletic stance is all about. Then have her jump into an athletic stance, followed by a dynamic drill by doing linked C-turns. If she still is having difficulty, start using ski tools that can assist her by remaining in balance and controlling her speed with poles, plastic hoops, or ski harness.

Challenge: A 64-year-old gentleman is having difficulty making and maintaining a wedge turn because of COPD and the lack of exercise.

Solution: Use a ski-tip connector to assist the senior with the weak leg muscles. Also, use a low-grade slope to provide him the opportunity to succeed to a higher self-esteem.

Challenge: This 72-year-old male senior is a Type 2 diabetic with hypertension. Being on diuretics, he has to go to the bathroom often.

Solution: After establishing bonding and trust and student-coach partnership, indicate to the student whenever there is an urgency, you will stop the lesson and allow him to go to the bathroom. Indicate to not be bashful or hesitant about this request. The coach will be mindful to remain close to the ski lodge so his client can get quick access to the bathroom. Challenge: This 78-year-old male student is out for the first time in over 20 years and has fear of the steep hills.

Solution: Assure him that his safety is your highest priority and concern. Based on his performance skill level, you will not only analyze whether he can perform on a particular slope, but also ask him if he will be comfortable on that hill. Also, we will also work on speed control by doing movement analysis to determine where the ineffective body movements are and substitute it with effective movements.

Challenge: This 72-year-old male wants to go from doing wedge turns to parallel turns.

Solution: By using the Ski Concept Model and Five Fundamentals of Skiing Mode he first starts with doing parallel turns after the fall line, and then before the fall line. Then he finishes by linking the parallel turns before and after the fall line.

Challenge: This 88-year-old woman's goal is to get some exercise outdoors. She indicated that she wants to be relatively disease free by eating healthy diets and get regular aerobic exercise to be physically and mentally fit.

Solution: Since she was not too keen about alpine skiing because her brother and sister both got into serious accidents, I decided to go with a more passive outdoor activity (i.e., Cross-country skiing) that offers aerobic exercise.

Photo 21. This woman loves the outdoors and the smell of the pine trees and mountain scenery while getting some exercise while cross-country skiing.

Challenge: A 51-year-old male is totally exhausted from this hour-long ski lesson because he failed to inform his instructor about his ongoing therapeutic sessions with chemotherapy and radiation.

Solution: This is something that you don't ever want to see. Because as one age: the chances of getting one or two diseases increases, you always want to inquire about their physical and cognitive development. You need to follow the Triple A Rule:

• A = Be Aware
• A = Be Alert
• A = Be Attentive

Photo 22. This athlete is dropping to the ground because of exhaustion and fatigue.

Challenge: A common error that is often committed is not staying in balance by pushing the shin forward to get the COM to be centered over the BOS.

Solution: Seniors like this game. I tell them that I will place a $100 bill between the shin and tongue of the snow boot; if he leans back the money will fly out and he will owe me the lost money (See figure 13).

Figure 12. The elderly love to laugh and have fun; try this game of putting money between the tongue of the boot and the shin and if your client sits back and lands on the heels of the feet the money will fly out and owes you some cash.

Challenge: A 63-year-old Asian woman that has a history of osteoporosis[23] but wants to learn how to ski with her children on their family vacations. Solutions: Being at high risk for broken bones, her beginner lessons should be on gentle hills with low-impact drills. Focus your drills on balance and try to use ski tools to help maintain her balance (e.g., Plastic hoops, ski poles, or ski harness).

Challenge: A 77-year-old man has dementia[23] and is having a hard time hearing[23] people even with his hearing aid.

Solution: First determine how severe is his hearing loss and so you can him so he can read your lips and the air movement of sound goes directly to I ears. Be sure to have him check if his hearing batteries are working and be sure that the background noise is not competing with both of your voices. W the dementia, also, stand directly in front of him and speak at a slower pace; repeat yourself often to ensure that he gets the message.

Challenge: You're having difficulty with your 69-year-old woman to stop filling the air with so much verbiage and unwanted conversation.

Solution: Try to understand some grandpa and grandma are somewhat lonely and are out to take a lesson to socialize. You can try to entertain them with your own 'war' stories, or fishing stories or hobbies (Gardening, horse training, golfing, sailing, music). The key thing to remember is to be patient and that their primary goal is to socialize.

Challenge: You have an 88-year-old client that keeps falling. Have a frank discussion to find out if it is a medical condition, medication, or combination of both that causing her to fall?

Solution: Once you obtained the facts, you can develop a teaching plan that will be safe your student. Work as partners. Falls can be very frustrating, demeaning, and dangerous. Be sure to provide feedback that is from the heart, accurate, and honest, yet diplomatic.

Challenge: An Elder 66-year-old client is habitual and may have difficulty doing new things or new movements.

Solution: Be patient and understanding of the situation. The hesitancy to change may be due to fear, which are collected as 'fear files' and stored in different parts of the brain over the years. At a certain point, the overfilled brain is paralyzed to make any new move. Do things in small steps and with movements that they are somewhat familiar with or someone in the group lesson that can do it without hesitation and see it as fun doing. Because nerve conduction slows down 40 percent in women over 70 -year-of-age, they lose confidence about falling. So, use a gentle terrain and go slowly.

This will certainly be a Terrain-Base Learning[21].

Challenging: A 82-year-old male is grumpy, old man who is complaining after the lesson that the progression of the lesson was not obvious and did not feel that he got his money worth.

Solution: It is desirable that Student and coach work on goals together as partners before even setting foot on the snow. Periodically, you need to ask your client if that scenario was what he was looking for and reflect that with positive feedback to build his self-esteem.

Challenge: This 51-year-old male amputee wants to learn racing techniques.

Solution: This advanced, senior skier hired an adaptive racing coach to learn the fundamentals of racing.

Photo 23. An adaptive skier that is an advanced-level performer, learning the fundamentals of racing.

Challenge: A 59-year-old male skier with lung cancer wants to learn parallel skiing during his chemotherapy and radiation therapy.

Solution: Because of the possible brittle bones as a consequence of the Brutal therapy, the coach put him on a wide open low-impact, gradual hill for his training. One of the major focuses should be the athletic stance. Most skiers lack that technique, the seniors especially because of arthritis and lack of flexibility and lack of exercise. A yoga instructor taught me two exercises that helped me with strengthening and increasing the flexibility of my ankle tendons, ligaments, and muscles. The first exercise was pointing the toe of each foot down and then up (For 15 minutes daily). The second drill is moving the toes clockwise and then counterclockwise for 15 minutes daily. In front of the mirror, the senior should emulate the perfect athletic stance (See Figure 5).

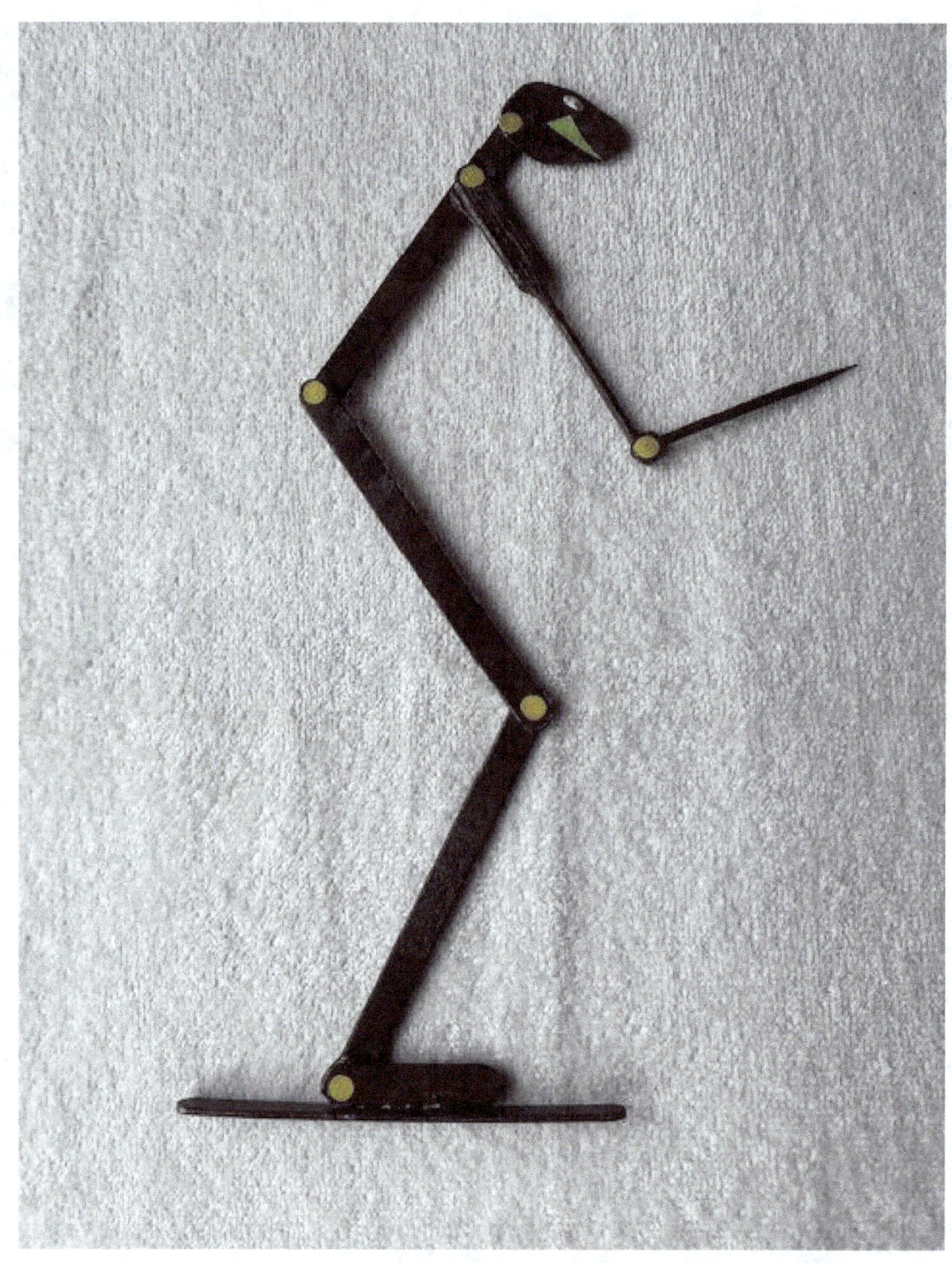

Figure 13. A stick drawing" of o perfect athletic stance. The ankles, knees and hip simultaneously flex so the COM moves forward. Notice that the 30 degree, bend of the upper torso matches the flex of the lower leg (Are parallel). To be in the balanced position, the COM must be centered over the BOS (Over the arch of the foot). The only difference with the senior citizens is their COM is higher because the bones should stack to be more efficient when they ski.

Challenge: This 57-year-old male want to have fun in the terrain park. Solution: After learning about the safety rules of the terrain park (SMART), he was taken to a less hazardous part of the park (Rolling hills and barrels) and taught the mechanics of skiing the rolling hills, the spine, the barrels. In summary, be mindful that as a senior specialist your responsibility is to simplify the lesson and achieve your client's goals and exceed customer satisfaction". Incorporate the Senior Specialist Teaching / Learning Cycle[21] to make the lessons easier to learn (See figure 3).

There are three major fundamentals to remember when teaching the seniors:

I) People Skills Fundamentals

• Develop relationships built on trust
• Engage in meaningful two-way communications
• Identify, understand, and manage your emotions and actions
• Recognize and influence the behaviors, motivations, and emotions of others

II) Teaching Skiils Fundamentals

• Collaborate on long-term goals and short-term objectives
• Manage information, activities, terrain selection, and pacing
• Promote play, experimentation, and exploration
• Facilitate the learner's ability to reflect upon experiences and sensations
• Adapt to the changes and needs of the learner
• Manage emotional and physical risksIII) The Five Alpine Fundamentals

• Control the relationship of the Center of Mass (COM) to the Base OfSupport (BOS) to direct pressure along the length of the skis
• Control pressure from ski to ski and direct pressure towards the outside ski
• Control edge angles through a combination of inclination and angulation• Control the skis' rotation (Turning, pivoting, steering, rotation, and separation from the upper body)

As I have mentioned numerous times in this book that the fear of falling by the elderly person and getting injured is a major concern. The cause of frequent falling is due to the *vestibulocochlear nerve* deeply imbedded in the foot going dormant after the age of 60 years-old. That can be corrected by reactivating this important nerve responsible for balance and stability.

Do this 10-minute exercise from your living-room couch; roll your feet over this hard ball with "spines" (See photo 24) daily to stimulate that nerve. Soon you will experience improvements with your balance and stability. Do share this important information with your senior citizen clients.

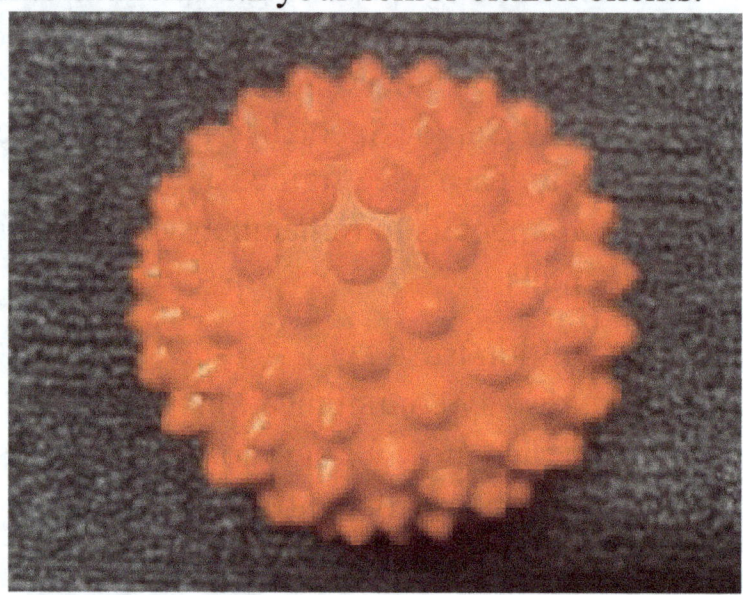

Photo 24. This hard-rubber ball with spines can be useful for exercising the soles of the foot (Vestibulocochlear nerve) to achieve better balance and stability, which is generally lost after age 60 years because that nerve goes dormant.

Chapter 10

Summary

Seniors are special people with unique set of circumstances. They have many ailments that affect their daily lives, which have an impact on any sport that they participate in. It takes a ski specialist that is knowledgeable about the senior's limitations and concerns.

The elders have concerns such as fear of falling, the impact of some of their diseases and medications. Their handicaps and limitations cause limitations of movements and execution of skills.

Natural falling causes additional concerns and considerations. However, many of these issues can be overcome with the specialized training and knowledge bottom-line success package. It is with this education that good things can happen when training these special folks.

Photo 25. To extend your evening on having fun, seek if there are any bands performing at the ski resort or nearby town.

One of the most valuable lessons for the elderly is learning how to get up effectively and efficiently with the use of a ski as a tool because of their loss of lean-muscle mass. If available, having another person to assist the getting-up process will be helpful. Be aware that when getting up, the senior person's back should always be facing to the side of the hill (Not downhill) to prevent any potential falling when getting up.

Welcome to the Magical World of Senior specialist Skiing!!!

References

1. Adaptive Alpine Technical Manual; PSIA Education Foundation,Lakewood, Colorado, 2017; 230 pages.

2. Adaptive Instruction Supplement: Diagnosis and MedicationClassifications; PSIA Education Foundation, Lakewood, Colorado, 2019; 80 pages.

3. Adaptive Snowsports Instruction; PSIA Education Foundation,Lakewood, Colorado, 2003; 108 pages.

4. Adult Alpine Teaching Handbook; PSIA; Vail and Beaver Creek Ski &Snowboard Schools; Beaver Creek, Colorado, 2011; 318 pages.

5. Alpine Handbook; PSIA Educational Foundation; Lakewood, Colorado,1996; 77 pages.

6. Alpine & Snowboard Teaching Handbook; Vail Resorts ManagementCo.; Vail, Colorado, 2004; 200 pages.

7. Alpine Technical Manual; PSIA; PSIA/AASI American SnowsportsEducation Foundation, Inc.; Lakewood, Colorado, 2014; 150 pages.

8. Brocksmith, Blake, Dorfman, Gary, and Lichterman, Douglas; How toPlay Harmonica: A Complete Guide for Beginners; Adams Media; New York, New York, 2018; 175 pages.

9. Children's Alpine Teaching Handbook; PSIA/AASI Intermountain (Northwest); American Snowsports Education Association; Lakewood, Colorado, 2010; 314 pages.

10. Children's Instruction Manual; PSIA Education Foundation; 1997; 151 pages.

11. Children's Instruction Manual, 21-Ici Ed.; PSIA Education Foundation;Lakewood, Colorado, 2008; 128 pages.

12. Core Concepts for Snowsports Instructors: Teaching; PSIA/AASIEducation Foundation; Lakewood, Colorado, 2008; 90 pages.

13. Cues to Ineffective and Effective Teaching; American SnowsportsEducation Foundation; PSIA, Educational Foundation, Lakewood, Colorado, 2008; 12 pages.

14. Herrin, Nicholas; "PSIA-AASI's Commitment to Snowsports Education: Is outlined in Best Practices for Teaching During COVID-19"; 32 Degrees; American Snowsports Education Foundation; Lakewood, Colorado, Fall 2020; pages 45-47.

15. Jay, Joshua; "Magic: The Complete Course; Workman PublishingCompany; New York, New York, 2008; 288. Pages.

16. Kazaniian, Kirk; Exceeding Customer Expectation; Random HousePublishing; New York, New York, 2007; 256 pages.

17. Maslow, A.; "A Theory of Human Motivation; Psychological Review;50:370-396 (1943).

18. New Snowsports Instructor Guide; PSIA/AASI Intermountain (West);PSIA Education Foundation; Lakewood, Colorado, Colorado, 2018; 27 pages.

19. Park and Pipe Instructor's Guide: Freestyle; PSIA/AASI AmericanSnowsports Education Foundation, 2005; 156 pages.

20. Pogue, David; "Magic for Dummies"; IDG Books Worldwide, Inc; NewYork, New York, 1998; 369 pages.

21. PSIAASI (Northwest); Senior Specialist Manual; American SnowsportsEducation Association, Inc., Lakewood, Colorado, 2018; 63 pages.

22. Snowboard Teaching Handbook; Product number 121PSIA EducationFoundation; Lakewood, Colorado, 2015; 358 pages.

23. Stanbury, John B., Wyngaarden, James B, Fredrickson, Donald S.,Goldstein, Joseph L. , Brown, Michael S.; The Metabolic Basis of

Inherited Disease; McGraw-Hill Book Company; New York, NY; 1983; 2032 pages.

24. Stadelman, Paul and Fife, Bruce; "Ventriloquism Made Easy";Piccadilly Books, Ltd.; Colorado Springs, Colorado, 2003; 108 pages.

25. Trueman, Bob; Ski in Control—How to Ski Any Piste Anywhere in FullControl: Man, Woman, Young or Old; Trueman Publishing Company, Roland Heights, California, 2017; 142 pages.

26. Teaching Snowsports Manual; American Snowsports EducationAssociation, Inc., Lakewood, Colorado, 1918; 262 pages.

27. Vail and Beaver Creek Children's Alpine Teaching Handbook; VailResorts Management Co.; Vail Colorado, 2004; 200 pages.

28. Wahba, A., and Bridgewell, L. "Maslow Reconsidered: A Review ofResearch on the Need of Hierarchy Theory; Organizational Research and Human Performance; 15: 212-240 (1976).

29. 2020 Ski Instructor Survival Guide; Deer Valley Ski Resort; Deer Valley, Utah, 2019; 206 pages.

30. 2020 ADA Standards of Medical Care in Diabetes; American Medical Association, Muncie, Indiana, 2019; 206 pages.

IN CLOSING, IN ORDER TO BE SUCCESSFUL SENIOR CITIZEN COACH WITH SKI LESSONS THAT ARE OUTSTANDING, YOU NEED TO DEVELOP A MIND THAT IS ELASTIC AND THAT CAN STRETCH TO MEET ALL THE NEEDS OF THE ELDERLY PERSON WHICH FOCUSES ON THEIR GOALS, THE THREE FUNDAMENTALS OF SKIING, THEIR MENTAL, SOCIAL, AND PHYSICAL DEVELOPMENTS, THEIR LIMITATIONS AS AN OLDER SKIER, KNOWING WHAT MOTIVATES THEIR LEARNING PROCESS, AND KNOWING HOW TO ACHIEVE CUSTOMER SATISFACTION TO THE MAXIMUM.

Notes

(1)

https://disabledATSdisabledsportseasternsierra.org

(2)

Ski Resorts Adjust, Hope Season Gets a Longer Run, "in USA Today, November 19, 2020, page 4D." during teaching a lesson.

US Review of Books

4.0 ★★★★☆

book review by Nicole Yurcaba

How to Create a Successful Ski Lesson for Senior Citizens

by Herbert K. Naito

"Continuous participation in alpine skiing past retirement age is a common one."

In this book, readers discover the skiing world as experienced by senior citizens. They learn how ski lessons can be a safe, active pastime for seniors. The book acknowledges that as a person age "the mind and body begin to falter." Readers also learn how skiing can be a therapeutic activity for those diagnosed with PTSD. The author highlights common medical conditions that may impact a senior citizen's skiing ability. However, he also gives the reader tips about navigating these ailments and enjoying a fruitful ski experience. As the book progresses, readers learn ski moves that match a senior citizen's physical ability, providing insights into how to adjust these movements according to need. Throughout the book, colorful photographs and graphics help readers better understand the material.

For ski coaches of any age, this book is important as more and more people of all ages focus on physical activity. The book provides discussions about how to provide for senior skiers, from beginners to advanced. The book encourages coaches to help skiers build and maintain confidence. Uniquely, the book also highlights the importance of skiing's social aspects, and it encourages coaches and instructors to be mindful about taking breaks and encouraging conversation within skiing groups. Thus, the book's section on methods of relaxation is important, especially in its emphasis on post -ski lessons and emotional, physical, and mental restoration. The book encourages readers to embrace this self -care practice in order to prevent harmful, even deadly, crashes. It also focuses on activities, like concerts, beyond the ski resort that skiers might enjoy.